Talking Walls:

Building Classroom Environments
to Support Student Achievement

By Michelle Karns and
Charlotte Knox

Dedication:

This book is dedicated to Katy and Arabella, our daughters, who often give us up so that we might spend time with other people's children. And to our mothers, Carma and Jean, who helped us understand the power of education and the importance of contributing to the quality of community.

Michelle Karns and Charlotte Knox

Talking Walls:
Building Classroom Environments
to Support Student Achievement

By Michelle Karns and Charlotte Knox

Knox Educational Associates, Inc.
534 Grandview Court
Point Richmond, CA 94801
Phone: 510-231-1900
FAX: 510-232-8049

To order additional copies of this book, go to www.knoxeducation.com

ISBN 978-1-4726-2423-9

First Printing August 2008

Acknowledgements

They say that "great teachers weren't born that way; they were created by the teacher next door...." It would not be possible to share this book with the educational community without the teachers whose work is represented in these photos. The pictures themselves were taken over a five-year period – 2003-2008 – during which we were consulting around the state in primarily Title I public schools.

We want to give special thanks to those teachers whose classrooms are represented with multiple photos. They took the ideas presented in our workshops and elsewhere and translated them into practices that worked for their students and themselves. Among these, special mention goes to Amanda Klein, Noah Bradley, Margarita Florez, Maria Sanner, Brenda Touhey, Ruben Olivares, and Julie Dulay of Think College Now in Oakland, California. This team has been working together with us for these five years to create classroom environments that support and extend learning for all students. Special thanks to Maureen Ferry and Kilian Betlach for sharing their middle school successes in the sections in this book entitled, "Portrait of a Middle School Classroom" and "5 Levers for Creating a Safe and Productive Learning Environment."

There have been a few extraordinary principals who have helped us be better at our jobs as education consultants: David Silver, Katie Curry, Sue Kaiser, Faye Sharpe, Maria Lewis, Janet Amani-Scott, and Bonnie Wilson. They have challenged us to constantly improve and determine the next steps to quality reform. They make our work responsive and connected to the real world.

Dennis Parker, our colleague and friend, needs to be acknowledged as a significant contributor to the process of change that led to the success experienced by all the schools featured. His reform model, Strategic Schooling, has shaped how these noted schools have been able to make significant gains in language arts and math. He also serves as a motivator and lead trainer for principals, teachers, and students. His phenomenal impact and his long white hair pulled into a braid down his back have made him a legend in California for more than 35 years.

The photos in the book come from all of the following schools and districts:

- Baldwin Academy, Fairgrove Academy, and Kwis Elementary in Hacienda La Puente Unified School District
- Freeman Elementary School in Woodland Joint Unified School District
- Hellyer School in Franklin McKinley Unified School District
- Hoover Elementary School in Redwood City Unified School District
- Kaseberg Elementary in Roseville City Schools
- Morgan Elementary School in Rialto Unified School District
- Olive View and Woodson Elementary schools in Corning Unified School District
- Patterson School in Vallejo City Schools
- Peres Elementary and Stege Elementary in West Contra Costa Unified School District
- Rosa Parks School in Berkeley Unified School District
- Tahoe Elementary and Jedediah Smith Elementary in Sacramento City Unified School District
- Think College Now, Melrose Academy, EnCompass, and International Community School in Oakland Unified School District
- Vineland School in Baldwin Park Unified School District

Judy Diaso, Berkeley Unified School district teacher and coach; and Madeleine Lee, Oakland Unified School district; were Charlotte's most important mentors during the first years of her teaching career. They taught the meaning of "classroom as sanctuary" and showed her how to put that into practice in her classroom.

Table of Contents

Table of Contents

Table of Contents

What You Will Find on Your CD

Item	Reference Page	File Name on CD
Bloom's Taxonomy Script	(78)	Bloom's Taxonomy Script.doc
Conversation Norms	90-99	Conversation Norms.doc
In the Perfect Classroom, We See, Hear, Feel…	97	In the Perfect Classroom-We See,-Hear-Feel.doc
Student Creed	100	Student Creed.doc
Reading Cake with Kindergarten Standards	(101)	Reading Cake with Kindergarten Standards.doc
Reading Cake with First Grade Standards	(101)	Reading Cake with First Grade Standards.doc
Reading Cake with Second Grade Standards	(101)	Reading Cake with Second Grade Standards.doc
Reading Cake with Third Grade Standards	(101)	Reading Cake with Third Grade Standards.doc
Choosing Just the Right Books	102-108	Choosing Just the Right Books.doc
5 Star Writing Checklists	109-113	5 Star Writing Checklists.doc
Tiered Vocabulary Blank Form	116	Tiered Vocabulary Blank Form.doc
Academic Language Sentence Stems Standards-Based (CDE)	(117)	G(x)_ELA_Acad_Lang_0208.pdf, G(x)_MATH_Acad_Lang_0208.pdf
Standards for the Week Form	118	Standards for the Week Form.doc
Kidified Standards-Grades K-6 Reading/Language Arts	(119)	Kidified Standards k-6-RLA.doc
Kidified Standards-Grades K-6 Math	(119)	Kidified Standards K-6-Math
Data Walls: Class Proficiency Charts, Mission 350 Chart, Student Score Cards	(121)	Class Proficiency Charts.xls, Mission 350 Chart.pub, Student Score Cards.xls
Benchmark Teacher Test Chat	122	Benchmark Teacher Test Chat.doc
Test Chat Samples	123-124	Test Chat 1.doc, Test Chat 2.doc
Other Data Sheets: 2nd Cold Read Bookmark, Scholar Math Vocabulary Chart	(125)	2nd Cold Read Bookmark.ppt, Class Proficiency Charts, Mission 350 Chart.ppt, Student Score Cards.doc
Skill Will Matrix	126	Skill Will Matrix.doc
Testing Word Cards	(127)	Testing Word Cards.doc
Bloom's Taxonomy Color Prompts	128-133	Bloom's Taxonomy Color Prompts.doc
Bloom's Taxonomy Student Work Sheet	135	Bloom's Taxonomy Student Work Sheet.doc
College Word Cards	(136)	College Word Cards.doc
Big Goal Award (Middle School Forms & Icons)	(137)	Big Goal Award.pub
3-in-1 Goal Icon (Middle School Forms & Icons)	137	3 in 1 Goal Icon.jpg
It Starts When You Walk Inside (Middle School Forms & Icons)	137	It Starts When You Walk Inside Icon.pub
Leave Your Mark Icon (Middle School Forms & Icons)	137	Leave Your Mark Icon.jpg
Sample Parent Letter on 3-in-1 Goal (Middle School Forms & Icons)	137	Sample Parent Letter on 3-in-1 Goal.pub
Big Goal 1, 2, 3, 4 (Middle School Forms & Icons)	138-141	Big Goal 1.doc, Big Goal 2.doc, Big Goal 3.doc, Big Goal 4.doc
Reading Non-Fiction – Types of Media (Middle School Forms & Icons)	147	Reading Non-Fiction – Types of Media.doc
Reading Non-Fiction – Text Features (Middle School Forms & Icons)	148	Reading Non-Fiction – Text Features.doc
Starters and Closers (Middle School Forms & Icons)	149-150	Starters and Closers.doc
Active Reader Strategies (Middle School Forms & Icons)	151	Active Reader Strategies.doc
Reading Strategies Goal Sheet (Middle School Forms & Icons)	152	Reading Strategies Goal Sheet.doc

Authors' Notes

Seeing is believing....

When I began teaching in Oakland, California in 1985 I noticed a big know-how gap between what I had been taught in my credential program and what my 32 southeast Asian first-graders seemed to need from me in order to understand what I was teaching. Nearly all of my students had arrived in the United States in the past couple of years and were classified as level 1 or 2 English learners. To help them, I simply had to start drawing pictures to go with the words I spoke and then put the pictures on the walls. I also learned from my mentor teacher, Judy Diaso, that if I used a lot of language experience charts instead of the literature-based basal reading program, my students would have access to reading material they could actually _read_. Soon, the walls of my classroom were covered with print and pictures. I noticed how the students would track those walls with their eyes as they attempted to participate in the daily lessons of school.

I will never forget the spring day when Dara, the confident boy pictured on page 29, came up to me during our writer's workshop to ask where the "Halloween word chart" was. I reminded him that Halloween was months ago, but found the chart hanging on our rack for him anyhow. As it turned out, he wanted to tackle writing a longer story for the first time and it was all about a ghost. He couldn't remember how to say that word in English, but he knew for certain that he could retrieve it from the Halloween word chart if he could get a look at the pictures again. I suddenly understood how essential all of those charts I drew were for these students. They needed them for their success. They had incredible memories for the locations of all the words they wanted to use in our classroom.

I have carried that experience with me for the past 12 years as I have been traveling the state supporting teachers in California schools with high percentages of English learners and students of poverty. I have tried to inspire teachers to likewise fill their rooms with English print that "holds still" for the students, so they can remember and retrieve all of the new language of school they are trying to learn and use during daily instruction. Words that are only spoken by the teacher or seen briefly in a book move out of view too quickly for these students. They need a holding ground to refer to over time. They need to know where to look when they can't recall a concept or term that is being used in the current lesson.

I provide workshops for teachers that give the background of a teaching strategy, model the strategy in action, and provide handout materials to which the teachers can refer. However, I have noticed that no matter how hard I work at making those workshops clear for the teachers, there is some difficulty in translating those new practices into their daily routine without "seeing" them in action with their own students. Ideally, I demonstrate each strategy "live" with the students. When this is not possible, I leave behind photos of the charts showing the strategies. Teachers will pour over these photos to see just how to illustrate their teaching for their students. They are also inspired by the many ways other teachers have found to embellish classroom charts with photos or pictures, adding color, and arranging information on the page.

I have been working with Michelle Karns for the past eight years. She has an amazing ability to read the research deeply and find ways to translate it into practice for daily teaching. I knew that when Michelle had the idea to organize and publish this book, based on the 5,000+ photos I have taken and shared with her over the years, she would help me find a way to do that as well. I am deeply grateful for her powerful mind, which seems to be able to hold so many pieces of information in a constellation that makes sense.

The goal for this book is to help teachers find ways to illustrate their instruction so that students can refer back to what was taught whenever they need to. The walls need to be set up to "talk" to the students about concepts and vocabulary, their own progress in school, and how the classroom community works together to make it a nurturing place for learning. I hope this helps. I am pretty sure it will!

Charlotte Knox

Folks,

After 30-something years in the business of helping students, schools, and families, I have become very aware of how important it is to share what we know to expedite helping our students learn. I think in *Talking Walls* we have something special to offer you. Charlotte wanted to share the classroom pictures and I wanted to focus on how the students were using their class-made content posters, vocabulary, grammar, and thematic materials, hence the book *Talking Walls*. I am convinced the *Walls* can become a powerful tool of collaboration between students and teachers. The walls "talk" when the students use them to revise, support, and review current academic work they are completing. The walls are "talking" when the students are writing and the walls prompt them on conventions, or help them select the appropriate academic language to describe a phenomenon, or even help them borrow a Tier II word for an essay.

Talking Walls is a labor and investment in sharing what we know, have observed, and have felt while working with your students in your classrooms. I believe that it is another way to make the teacher tool kit and the know-how of teachers expand. Charlotte is a great mentor. You can trust her instructional recommendations. She has a great classroom demeanor and organizational style.

I am the great observer. You can be assured that this *talking walls* phenomenon exists and that many teachers are using it to benefit students. It is serendipitous that the students seeming to gain the greatest benefit are the students with whom we have the greatest difficulty moving toward proficiency. But I like that we have stumbled onto something that is helpful, although the strategy is not new. Perhaps the methods, content, and intensity of how we recommend that you use *Talking Walls* is unique, but GLAD (Guided Language Acquisition Design) strategies facilitated a similar protocol for years.

I hope you enjoy what we have done. Please embark on a picture-taking journey with your students and start asking them if the walls are "talking." I can guarantee if the walls aren't talking, the students will be talking about you. Just give them my e-mail and I will explain everything.

Michelle Karns
Aka "Miss Michelle"

Talking Walls

Introduction: Listening to the Walls

Talking Walls started as a concept after we noticed students using what was posted on the walls as prompts for their current work and projects. From using the sound spelling cards to decode words that were unfamiliar to trying to see the board for the homework assignment, students were constantly looking around the classroom to figure out what to do and how to do it. Whether it was accessing the tiered vocabulary listing to capture another word for "beautiful" or looking for a quick icon to remind them about the meaning of the preposition "toward," the walls seemed to "talk" to some of the students.

When a student was asked how he used the vocabulary word cards that were posted in the classroom on the theme wall, he said, "I let them talk to me." He went on to say that after they were on the walls for awhile he seemed to know them. When asked how he thought that happened, he replied that, "I use them all the time. I look at them and think of ways to use them, and I think of ways to shock people that I know the words." He also said that his teacher put up student work that was "really good" so you had to pay attention to the walls. "They were always talking." After this dialog, we started to look for walls that "talked" and students with whom they spoke. Our first interviewee was correct. Other students heard the walls.

And then there were classrooms where the walls failed to talk at all. They were covered with published posters and neat borders. Everything had a place and it wasn't always clear where the students fit in. Sometimes it wasn't clear that students resided in the room six to seven hours a day. When we looked at the data produced on formative and summative tests, it was clear that certain demographic groups got left out of the process in the classrooms without "talking walls." Could closing the gap be as simple as encouraging students to use the visual prompts that they created from interactive processes?

Spending 10-20 hours a week observing what happens in classrooms for the last 10 years gives an interesting perspective to what needs to happen. We acknowledge that most consultant types go in and look at the behavior of the teachers. They check the instructional methods, the tone, evidence of an effective learning community, and depending on the bias of the observer, the checklist goes on.

We prefer to watch the students. We have a whole host of questions that we filter through in a flash: How are the students engaged? What kinds of questions are they asking? How are they answering the questions being put forth? Do they use full sentences? Casual or formal register? Tier I or II vocabulary? Academic language? Do they know protocol? Do they have their materials? Homework? Repartee? Laughter? Any evidence of emotion or meaningfulness? Connections to prior learning? Are they using terms congruent with the lesson objectives? Do they reflect the standards in their language? Do the students respond as if the teacher is "WITHIT"? (Kounin, 1970)

As we looked at the children who used the walls, we noticed a trend. They were also the students who needed the extra support. The walls had become a resource for them. This was consistent with a number of researchers who found that the classroom environment needed to complement instruction, support the culture of the achievement, and underscore the long-range goals. We used a prescription that recommends a 30-30-30 model. Thirty percent of the classroom displays and postings need to reflect the current themes and instructional targets. Thirty percent needs to be committed to student work and present the evidence of achievement. Thirty percent should be dedicated to the overall grade-level standards and academic objectives, especially the key outcomes. The extra ten percent should reflect the teacher. We recommend a teacher corner – family, degrees, pictures of the dog, and personal goals. Maybe even a picture of your first day as a teacher and now.

Introduction: Listening to the Walls

We saw the darnedest thing during testing for the CST. Even when the materials were covered for testing, the students still looked to that area of the room, closed their eyes, and *visualized* what was once there. We are not sports aficionados, but it is said that Tiger Woods does the same thing playing golf. Visualization is a dimension of success on most athletes' lists. We are now putting it on the list for academic athletes. We call it visual literacy – the capacity to see. This "seeing" could be a definition via an icon or remembering a story based on the leftover feelings that are conjured in a picture of an old woman. Visual literacy is about symbols and how we respond and interpret meanings from our experiences. Varied experiences make for different meanings.

Education helps make meanings more congruent and establishes some norms. It doesn't tell us that we can't use words in our own way, just that everyone might not understand. It is just one of the weirdnesses of the English language. Using the language is what is valuable. The students need to talk – meaningfully – about learning.

Learning-Focused Conversations

Learning-focused conversations can be the foundation of the change process that closes the achievement gap! It is the means to bring students who have otherwise been left out of continuous achievement into a success experience. Learning becomes a product of the dance between what the student knows, what we help them learn, and what they discover from their learning partners in conversations. (See www.knoxeducation.com for full explanation and set of cards).

The **basic elements of a Learning-Focused Conversation**:

- It is a person-to-person *verbal* exchange.
- Neither person has greater power than the other. That is, no one in a conversation is *judged* to be superior or valued as more important.
- Common language or the *casual register* is used.
- Both people *get to talk* in a conversation. Neither side tells the other what to *do* or how to *feel.*
- The ideal is that new *information* is shared, or an exchange of perspectives occurs, or that a problem is resolved.

The *learning-focused conversation* starts a process that validates the student and his or her connection to what happens in the classroom. It is a vital process and can keep students hooked into school.

Learning-Focused Conversations Cards

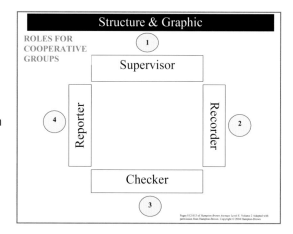

Introduction: Listening to the Walls

Student Work

Creating evidence of learning is an opportunity to demonstrate how the student has internalized the lesson. All students filter a lesson their own way through background knowledge, family experiences, cultural biases, and prior learning.

Any time that student work is displayed it is recommended that the performance standard(s) it meets are also posted with the presentation. Whenever possible, the actual assignment can also be noted next to the student work. Post-it® notes can be provided for observers to leave feedback if the display warrants comments.

Other people help us see things we are unable to see; they can report progress, give feedback, let us know how we are doing, and provide another perspective that may open our own eyes. Without others' feedback and involvement, it is not likely that we can improve or change in a timely manner.

When we display student work, we are saying to the student, their parents, and any classroom visitor:

- This work is valued in this classroom.

- The effort put forth to complete this work met or exceeded expectations.

- The student really understands that this is a very important concept or skill. The concept or skill is part of what has to be learned at this grade level or for this class.

- This work meets the current instructional target and needs to be validated!

If education is our business, students are our clients, and their work is the evidence that we have effectively made a connection. Connections can increase or improve a skill, develop content knowledge, and foster the ability to think critically. When students start to notice how what they know helps them learn what they don't know they begin to understand the concept of building knowledge.

Displaying student work makes the learning and knowledge visible. It makes it stand still so that the teacher and student can examine the concepts or skills that are being taught.

The Evidence Project at Harvard demonstrated that student work is an important "window into children's thinking and learning." When teachers collaborate and review student work together, they are better able to understand the connections between the lesson plan, actual instruction, performance goals, and student production.

Communicate to the students that their efforts matter. It is a vital message that can validate the personal choices and control over learning environment. They can be in control of their learning by focusing their attention on doing the best job possible in their own way. Being in control of learning puts the student in a very important driver's seat; it can change the trajectory of their entire lifetime.

Classroom as Sanctuary

The best classrooms are learning sanctuaries. They provide refuge, a safe place for all kinds of thinkers, learners, and producers. To do this well, the sanctuary must place value on all who enter and underscore that differences are accepted. We always recommend that every student should be known by name within the first week of school and that the teacher should strive to have at least one personal fact about the student stored away from those first interactions. Writing positive personal notes home to parents during the first three weeks of school will create a prosocial connection between school and home that will withstand most adversity. From this connection, teachers can gain important cooperation for attendance, homework, and academic supports.

Anyone walking into the prosocial classroom will know what kind of teacher guides the students; what the students are learning and why; and how the students feel about their learning experiences. The classroom walls can introduce the student and visitors to how the classroom operates.

The classroom is comfortable but remains a learning environment. One of the ways this happens is through the students' awareness about cultural differences, silence norms, and conflict training for problems that arise when people disagree or perceive things differently. Agreements for interactions are established early on in an effective classroom. One of the ways to quickly establish norms is to take the classroom through the "perfect classroom" debriefing.

For example, ask the students what the "perfect classroom" would look like, sound like, or feel like. Chart the responses. Then ask, "What would it take to create the conditions in the classroom to make these things happen?" "Are any of these things similar?" "Can any be collapsed together?"

Distill fewer than five agreements that will lead to the "perfect classroom." Challenge the students to agree. When they do agree, post the agreements and use them daily for all process-oriented events. Make them a part of all decision-making procedures and protocol. When a disruption occurs, use the rules to describe what went wrong, or call out what you are seeing before a problem occurs. For example, "I am seeing people fail to take turns talking. Let's honor our agreements."

(Find the "In the Perfect Classroom" on page 107 in the Tool Kit and on the CD.)

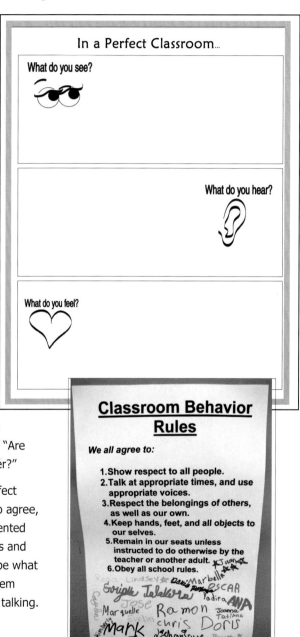

In a Perfect Classroom...

What do you see?

What do you hear?

What do you feel?

Classroom Behavior Rules

We all agree to:

1. Show respect to all people.
2. Talk at appropriate times, and use appropriate voices.
3. Respect the belongings of others, as well as our own.
4. Keep hands, feet, and all objects to our selves.
5. Remain in our seats unless instructed to do otherwise by the teacher or another adult.
6. Obey all school rules.

Classroom as Sanctuary

The Challenge of Providing Sanctuary

The challenge of providing sanctuary goes beyond opening doors and letting people in to the refuge or the "safe place." We believe that the sanctuary safety in the classroom is grounded in the quality of the relationship between teachers and their students. The effective teacher-student relationship is framed by the understanding that productive learning is engendered by a positive emotional experience and is triggered by meaningful connections. Emotions and meaningfulness are the driving forces behind any sustained interest or desire to learn. These elements are also rationales for why you might seek refuge in the classroom. If you feel safe there and if what happens there is meaningful, you will seek sanctuary in a classroom over and over again.

Sociologists maintain that humans will always do what benefits them. For children or young people to select school as a place of sanctuary, they will require beneficial experiences and people of influence helping them make the connections. The benefits of behavior are usually easily determined after a period of observation of a child or youth in a variety of interactions. Then, the real challenge is to replicate the perceived benefit in prosocial terms and reinforce the new behavior until the benefit of the antisocial behavior becomes extinct.

Behavior	Behavioral Benefit
Disrespect, teasing, disturbing the class, being uncooperative, swearing, talking, being out of their seat, and making fun of others	**Attention**
Disobeying, disrespect, not cooperating, talking back, disturbing the class	**Power**
Bullying, shoving, pushing, teasing, causing embarrassment, excluding others	**Revenge**
Not paying attention, not being prepared, being dishonest, wasting time	**Avoidance of Failure**

(adapted from Dr. Rudolph Dreikurs, 1968)

Classrooms as Safe Haven

A chaotic classroom has the students experiencing highs and lows to the point of emotional overload. For students who live in uncertainty, chaos in the classroom thwarts the learning environment and sabotages the students.

Many youth relate negative, frustrating experiences between home and school to mean that they must behave in an aggressive manner at school. We challenge teachers to create every classroom as a safe haven. Reinforce for students that the classroom can be different from how you act at home or in the neighborhood.

A predictable schedule and routine helps students relax and focus on learning. The agenda and schedule provide an instructional timeline for students. They provide the organizational structure that makes it clear what will happen throughout the course of the day. The agenda and schedule literally set the stage for teaching and learning. They let students know that the teacher is in charge and will be able to take care of the day's events.

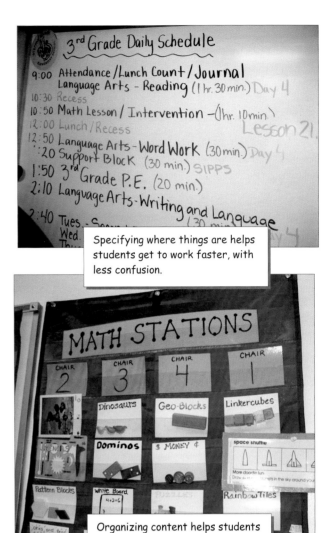

Specifying where things are helps students get to work faster, with less confusion.

Organizing content helps students coordinate their efforts.

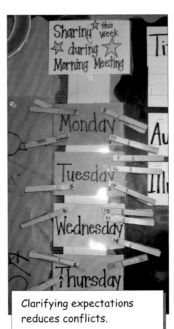

Clarifying expectations reduces conflicts.

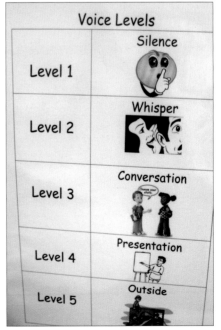

Classrooms and Predictability

Predictability is needed for high-risk, high-need, and highly emotional students. It provides the safety to be open to learning and the conditions necessary to sustain focus.

Rules and protocol are important in the classroom; they help the group to function in acceptable and organized ways. Adherence to the rules shows *respect* and *consideration* for others.

The more simple the rules and protocol, the more likely they will be managed well and not forgotten. It is imperative that they be practiced. Tests can even be given to check for understanding.

It is assumed that over time, all of the students will remember the rules and protocol. This is not true! Bring the process up over and over again. Even 30 days after the students have assimilated the rules and protocol as norms, schedule a review. Make up songs or chants for your classroom. A "creed" can integrate all of your expectations. *(See Tool Kit, page 110, and CD for sample of Student Creed.)*

There need to be places assigned for classroom routines that require quick transitions: collecting homework; accessing available materials such as paper, pencils, and sharpeners; getting textbooks; selecting library books for free and voluntary reading; or accessing dictionaries, thesauruses, and other resources.

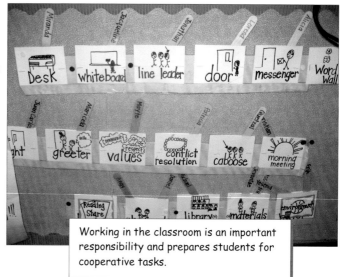

Working in the classroom is an important responsibility and prepares students for cooperative tasks.

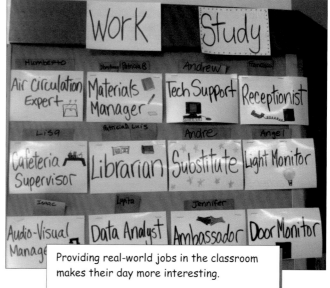

Providing real-world jobs in the classroom makes their day more interesting.

Showing students what you expect for their space at school helps them remember and makes it more likely to happen! Keeping things organized by team is helpful with these inexpensive shelf units.

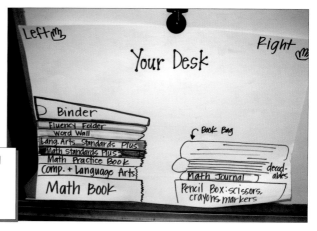

Classrooms Are for Students

It is never too late to have a childhood or to become a student. It is, however, the teacher's responsibility to create the conditions to make it happen for those students who have not had successful experiences in the past.

You would not expect someone who has never driven a car to drive well. They may have ridden in the car, seen cars in motion and observed people driving, but an expectation that they could drive well would be a set-up for their failure. Many children don't know "how" to be students. Their parents may not be literate, they may have moved repeatedly, or they may not have had a teacher invested in their success.

An effective teacher-student relationship and quality classroom walls can help set students up to succeed. They can provide students with information that they might not have in their personal repertoire of prior experiences. The walls can provide clues of what needs to be done to be successful in current academic tasks. They can offer the models and information to meet current educational targets based on the standards. The wall can help students to *see* that the goal is attainable and not an ambiguous target that only the "smart kids" can understand. *The classroom walls are an extension of the teacher-student relationship and commitment to helping every student succeed.* This relationship has great influence and is a significant motivator.

For example, we have interviewed students who have "gained" more than one proficiency level in a single year. These "gainers" all reported a common experience for the year of extraordinary learning, "My teacher told me I could do it." "I really liked my teacher." "My teacher was so cool, she was the best teacher I ever had." And when we checked with the teachers, they said, "He was the best kid." "I had to really work with him." "She really worked with me." The students work hard because of their relationship with the teacher.

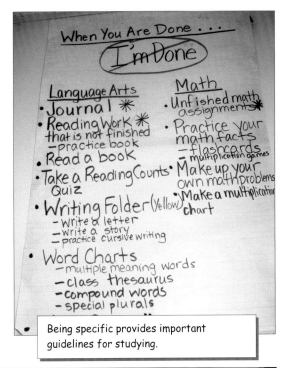

Being specific provides important guidelines for studying.

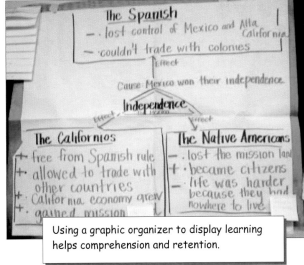

Using a graphic organizer to display learning helps comprehension and retention.

Using more rigorous strategies at all ages is imperative.

Classrooms are Like Stage Sets

Classroom arrangements are like stage sets. As the teacher, you are designing the set for maximum exposure to a learning center.

They are also like staging a dinner party. You have to place your guests in optimum seats so they will have meaningful conversations that will not distract from the main event, which is learning. Finally, classrooms are like laboratories. Everything that happens is both experimental and planned. It is organic and process-oriented.

The way the room is arranged often contributes to results. Paying attention to the classroom set-up is imperative. Here are a few questions to ask. "Yes" answers mean you are on the right track:

- Can every student see the information that supports your instructional goals?

- Can the students see the standards?

- Are your English learners close to you and able to see your expressions?

- Do you have a space that can function as a safe, comfortable, time-out place?

- Is there student work posted meaningfully?

As the teacher, you have many roles. You are the director of the play, host of the daily event, and the scientist creating the conditions to test the process outcomes. The key challenge is that you are constantly monitoring and adjusting to ensure that your students are participating at their highest levels possible.

Organizing classrooms with ready-made libraries gives immediate access to print for free time.

Providing an inviting corner of the classroom for independent reading motivates K-5 students to want to pick up a book.

Hint: Asking retail outlets for free or low-cost display shelves such as this one can help students see the covers of the books as they are selecting.

Classrooms for Reinforcement

Too often, celebrating with students takes the form of a bribe for a specific behavior. Reinforcement does not always have to be <u>extrinsic</u>, although it certainly works for a period of time with certain groups of students. Rewards that "stick" with students are those that are emotionally tagged; the <u>intrinsic</u> rewards. The intrinsic rewards are often the little things – sharing lunch together, letting a student read your book, asking a student for help, giving positive feedback, or writing a special note on their paper.

Below is a display of all the awards won outside of school by students in a single fifth-grade classroom. This was the teacher's way to say, "We are winners already!" It was a daily reminder that everyone in the class has a winning background. The display is a metaphor for expectations in the classroom. If students see themselves as a successful class it is easier to challenge them to higher expectations.

We value acknowledgement of all kinds, but are especially fond of using photos. Children living in poverty seldom have the pictures that many middle-class families have of their children. In fact, some of our newest immigrant students reported that their families have <u>no</u> pictures of them. So we started recommending that our teachers take pictures of their students and post them next to the students' work. After posting the pictures, give them to the students for home displays.

A powerful intrinsic acknowledgement is simply writing a note reporting how much you value the student and her or his learning. Nothing is better than a positive note from a teacher! During home visits, parents often proudly display teacher notes home on their refrigerator for all to see. Add pictures and you've made an ally forever.

Creating a mural as a final project helps students collectively determine all that they learned.

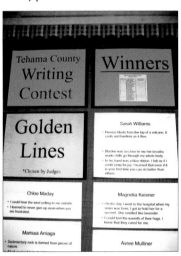

Providing a place in the classroom to display awards reminds students that they are winners. Champions of all kinds are celebrated within the classroom.

Classrooms as a Prosocial Place

Teachers make the difference in the classroom sanctuary. Students feel safe because the teachers have made it clear that they will honor the rule to protect their right to be there. No one will make fun of them for what they <u>don't</u> know. In the sanctuary, we will celebrate what they <u>do</u> know.

Working prosocially with others is a key ingredient to a dynamic classroom. This is a significant marker that the classroom has changed. We used to teach students in rows and the teacher lectured. There was little interaction or student engagement. Some students got the information, and many did not. That's the way it was. There was no expectation that *everyone* would be highly educated.

Most students need their peers and teachers. They desire feedback and like the repartee of being with others. If all humans could tolerate doing school with just a computer and the Internet, they'd be on their own. Thank goodness we have not figured out how to replace the responsiveness of teachers and the interaction with peers.

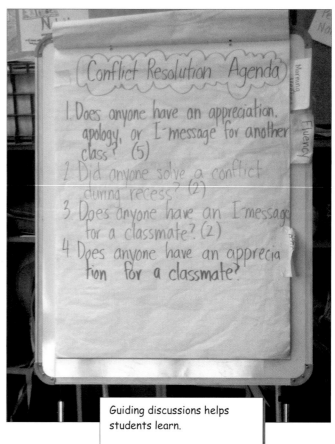

Guiding discussions helps students learn.

Sharing good books helps ensure comprehension.

Using small groups gives teachers personal time with students.

Classrooms for Relationships

Optimistic and future-focused youth will learn more than students who are impacted by stress and the resulting hormone, cortisol. Comfort, safety, and a sense that you are cared about all contribute to the necessary emotional experiences that promote a healthy and productive learning environment.

We say these types of experience are within the **WILL** domain, or the arena that is framed by the relationships between the teacher and the students, teacher and parents, students to students, teacher to teacher, and administrator to teachers and students. While it may seem like a cliché, it is the absolute truth that **relationships matter** at school.

All of the reform literature about successful schools serving diverse, minority, and socioeconomically challenged families indicates that successful schools embrace their students and families as truly capable and competent. They operate from a strength paradigm instead of the deficit model. Success in reform is **WILL**-based, which sets the stage for **SKILL building** and **growing knowledge**.

(See the Skill Will Matrix on page 135 of the Tool Kit and on the CD.)

Making every child stand out as an individual is part of the prosocial campaign, "Every child by name."

Laughing students are ready to learn.

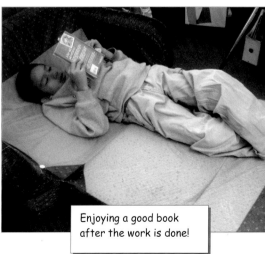

Enjoying a good book after the work is done!

Collaboration

Student collaboration prepares youth for a lifetime of successful work, team participation, and family interaction. To make collaboration successful in the classroom, there are three basic agreements: We are clear about our goals; we trust each other to do the shared work; we celebrate our efforts and our success.

In a group, everyone accepts a variety of roles and tasks. These roles demand that members work hard and fairly, and share resources. The tasks need to be completed without errors. An important aspect of being part of a collaborative group is sharing responsibility without causing conflict or hurting others intentionally.

Most students understand the value of teamwork and can learn the pleasure of working together in a positive environment. There are two key strategies: collaboration and cooperation. Collaboration is what we do when we work together and produce something; cooperation describes how we do it.

Collaboration simply describes being with others and working toward a common goal. Everyone offers and contributes. All team members in the collaborative group make the "we" come before "me."

The act of cooperation is a group process that targets working together without threats of violence, bullying, or unresolved conflict. The cooperative group will be focused on an integration of ideas and effort. Students begin to hunger for the feeling of satisfaction that comes from membership in a unique group.

Musicians understand collaboration and cooperation well. They know that in order to create a good sound, everyone must play their own part the best they can and listen to the others.

Valuing students working together focuses on the process, not the outcome.

Engaging partnerships give children the opportunity to invest in one another's success.

Collaboration

Collaboration and cooperation are a dynamic learning process as students in the classroom develop investment in one another. These strategies can become the means to explain the ethical and moral imperatives inside a classroom. If collaboration is a norm, then certain forms of communication are required: active listening, paraphrasing, speaking one at a time, allowing others to put their ideas on the table, using no put-downs, and working out conflicts. Consensus would be an expectation.

Cooperation conjures another set of descriptors: kind, helpful, other-focused, thoughtful, and being a contributor. Those who cooperate give of themselves for a common and shared goal.

Student-made work shows cooperation and collaboration. Could these products have been completed without these skills? We don't think so. In fact, our experiences have helped us understand that children need classrooms that promote collaboration and cooperation so they might experience a culture of acknowledgement and competence. Competence is the third "C" in the triangulation of student success. Through the process of collaborating and cooperating, students achieve a shared goal that helps them build the capacity for competence.

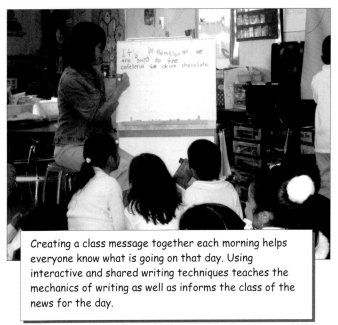

Creating a class message together each morning helps everyone know what is going on that day. Using interactive and shared writing techniques teaches the mechanics of writing as well as informs the class of the news for the day.

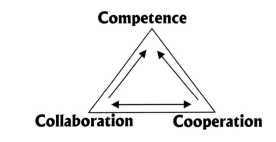

Competence

Collaboration   **Cooperation**

Arranging furniture so that students can work in teams and keep track of their books and supplies on a common shelf is really helpful. The student desks in this room are divided by inexpensive bookshelves – one per team.

Providing opportunities for student performances helps to develop skills and interests that may not be available in the home environment or experience.

The Literate Environment: The Reading Cake

By now the story of the development of the "reading cake" is a professional urban legend in our neighborhood. We will tell the story as we know it to be true. Dr. Jim Sweeney, then Superintendent of Sacramento City Unified School District, asked his principals and reading coaches to explain how to teach reading using phonics. One really talented coach and principal, Katie Curry, explained that is was like the layers of a birthday cake, each layer relying on the one before it to hold it up. The layers were: concepts of print, phonics, fluency, vocabulary, comprehension and on top were the candles or benefits of reading! In the audience that day was Aida Molina, a principal. She pondered the Curry cake and took it to her staff slightly modified. Then the National Reading Panel (NRP) declared that all programs for reading had to have five discrete elements: phonemic awareness, phonics, fluency, vocabulary, and comprehension—which matched the Molina cake!

As the coach for Ms. Molina, I (Michelle) took the cake and separated each layer into the discrete skills defined by the NRP. Then Aida Molina decided the cake needed a plate, I made the plate a "sea of talk" as Marie Clay would

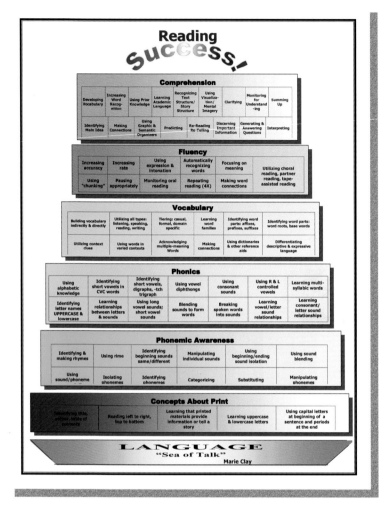

prescribe according to colleague, Dennis Parker (Strategic Schooling). I can hear him, "Language is only developed when the child is surrounded by rich interactions, opportunities to talk and experiments with language." Many of the children we serve have been dealt "puddles of talk" not "seas". It is therefore predictable that their language skills are underdeveloped and sometimes delayed—they haven't been jump-started yet. School is, for many youth, going to be the language environment to provide the most productive experiences for listening, speaking, writing, and reading. That is why our cake has the "concepts of print" layer while the National Reading Panel no longer lists it among the basics.

We have included *(in the Tool Kit, page 111, and on the CD)* the multi-layered cake that matches the National Reading Panel recommendations, defines the discrete skills, is grounded in language experience, and is color coded. If a student isn't successful at one level, you can look for the skill that needs to be addressed at the current level or look at the layer below. It is like a quick map to reading skills. Ms. Molina has even attached the standards to the cake layers for grade levels from K-3. She is very instructionally focused and plans with her teachers how they will meet the standards in our program called the Academic Conference. We have included the K-3 cakes on the CD for other teachers or administrators that want to make sure their K-3 students are meeting the English Language Arts (ELA) objectives and standards.

Parents really like the cake and it seems to help them understand reading conceptually. It is a great tool at conferences so that parents can start to focus practically on the skills that need to be targeted for children who are under performing.

The Literate Environment:
Prompts for Learning

Simplifying the process helps.

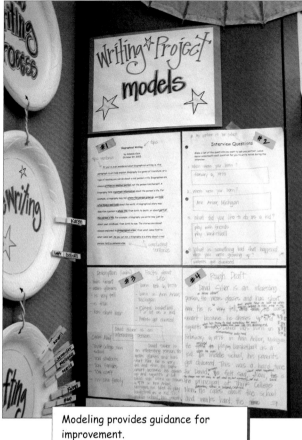

Modeling provides guidance for improvement.

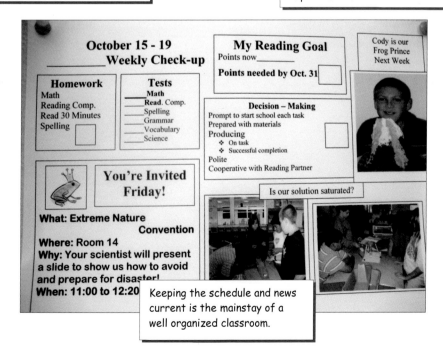

Keeping the schedule and news current is the mainstay of a well organized classroom.

The Literate Environment:
The Culture of Reading and Writing

Print poverty is a common symptom in the homes of children who have trouble learning to read. Without access to print and little experience with recreational reading a student will have difficulty beginning the interactions that make up literacy.

All too often teachers confuse lack of experience with print with lack of ability in reading. Children who are regularly read to can enter kindergarten having "read" 1500 books, while children who don't have books in their homes may have had next to none.

Along with language itself, a student must also be given access to newspapers, magazines, fliers, comics, paperbacks, hardbacks, and handwritten stories. They need a framework to hang their new lessons on that relates to the world they live in. They must learn to integrate the culture of books and print into their lives.

The ancient art of conveying events is an important and valid component in the education of a literate mind. Many students in our most challenged K-2 classrooms have never had a relationship with books or storytelling. When students tell stories that are well known in their families, they become recorders *and* reporters of their family history. The oral tradition can be written and bound to the literate tradition. These narratives can become a part of the classroom library, making everyone's oral traditions valuable to the classroom culture.

Ways we choose books...
- if I think I will enjoy it
- look at the cover
- pick a book in a series or set
- reading books by the same author
- reading recommended books
- flip through the pages
- read some of the words to see if they are interesting
- reading the title
- by reading the back cover and the inside flap
- looking at the pictures in the book
- characters we enjoyed reading about before

Helping students understand the thinking processes around choosing a book to read is an important aspect of learning how to read for fun. Avid readers do this with automaticity; others need to be shown how to select a book just right for them.

(See Tool Kit and CD for the strategy "Choosing Just the Right Books," page 112-118.)

Displaying classroom books in baskets by level, topic, and genre helps students make the best selections for voluntary reading.

The Literate Environment:
The Culture of Reading and Writing

"Reading makes you smart and writing makes you smarter!"

In a reading campaign meeting with the principal, a third grader exclaimed, "Mrs. Molina! I think I get it! Reading makes you smart, but writing makes you smarter!" "Yes!" said Mrs. Molina. In fact, this third grader had simplified a very complex issue for the staff – how to integrate reading and writing easily. This became the new slogan for the campaign. The goal was to read one million words. Research tells us that reading at this level will influence vocabulary, fluency, and comprehension. We were going to help the students read a million words by writing more.

Students, using the tools given, became engaged in writing and improved their formative testing. As evidence of their improvement was documented through the colorful exhibition of data, recreational reading in the classroom increased. The students didn't have to be pushed or pulled. Instead, it was the learning model itself that created change.

Using strategies to organize data is an important learning tool. For example, sticky notes help students keep track of what they are learning as they read. The notes can later be moved to a graphic organizer or a classroom chart to show group learning.

We always thought that English learners had to develop their fluency to read before they could write. We were surprised to find that, with the increased focus on writing, reading skills improved. They were motivated to work on vocabulary, which heightened comprehension.

Of course this makes sense. Writing gently demands the skills needed to read, but it offers an insider's perspective. Through the *process* of writing, the student begins to understand and put into action the integration of conventions and mechanics, creativity, and genres. This leads to a finished product that can be edited by its author and shared with peers. The student then actively documents progress and enjoys the satisfaction of a final product that can be published!

Displaying favorite books by making a card listing the title and authors for others to see contributes to an active recreational reading campaign inside the classroom.

The Literate Environment: Vocabulary and Content

Students need to have multiple and frequent experiences with a word to make it their own. They need to 1) *see the word* in order to 2) *think about it*. Once they see it and think about it, they can 3) *use it* productively. Activities in vocabulary need to bring these three stages into play so that they can begin to understand the word and practice with it. Knowing words that you don't apply to your daily conversation or your school work makes learning them have no value. So don't ask your students to learn vocabulary that you don't validate. Also, please don't require them to look words up in the dictionary and write sentences. This is busy work and, according to the research, doesn't expand vocabulary. This is one of our personal campaigns.

Vocabulary instruction needs to be explicit and active. It should be exciting to learn the nuances of language. To be exciting it has to be engaging. The students need you to be involved in this meaningful process. This is well worth your time.

Gains in vocabulary can change your IQ! Students literally get smarter! (We know this also relates to the testing instruments and how we assess IQ.) How does this happen? Increases in vocabulary provide increased comprehension. Like reading and writing, vocabulary and comprehension are reciprocal.

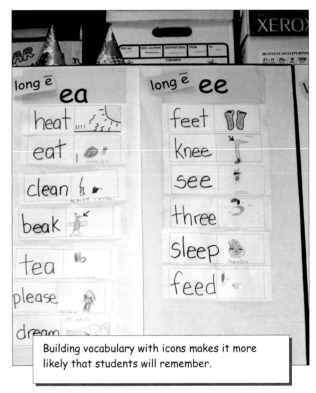

Building vocabulary with icons makes it more likely that students will remember.

Helping students with unknown words starts by making this task explicit. Bridging the "known to the new" always helps.

Using white boards for review of vocabulary words helps cement the learning.

The Literate Environment: Vocabulary and Content

Steven Stahl and T. Gerard Shiel state in their article, *Teaching Meaning Vocabulary,* that vocabulary instruction requires three basic strategies:

- Deriving meaning from context
- Teaching word parts
- Teaching words as part of semantic groups

Stahl and Shiel maintain that children can learn about 3,000 new words each year. Poor readers only learn about 1,000 words each year. Teachers only teach 300-400 words explicitly. The expectation is that most vocabulary will be generated from reading and dialogues with literate people. Poor readers seldom do either. The only way to move them up is to increase direct instruction.

Increasing direct instruction will require that you first check to see if there are other problems getting in the way of their reading: Does the student have all their letters and sounds? Phonological awareness? Base vocabulary? Conventions and mechanics?

After you get a good read of the basics, then move forward on creating a plan that will increase direct instruction in a smaller group.

Giving students opportunities to "see" the story helps retention, comprehension, and sequencing.

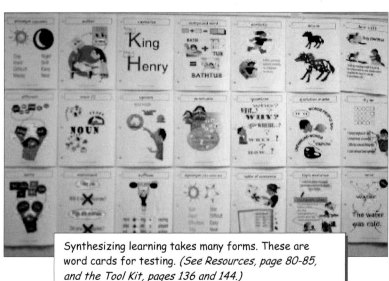

Synthesizing learning takes many forms. These are word cards for testing. *(See Resources, page 80-85, and the Tool Kit, pages 136 and 144.)*

Making complex information visual also makes it comprehensible.

The Literate Environment: Vocabulary and Content

There are two levels of vocabulary – the words that we can identify and understand in print and those we recognize from speech. This is called receptive and productive vocabulary. Receptive vocabulary is what we can hear and say, while productive vocabulary is what we can read and write. These are often different, depending on the parents' level of education and students' experiences.

Students need experiences with both types of vocabulary within the classroom to cement the word knowledge into their personal lexicon. Once they commit a word to their lexicon, it is forever accessible. It is theirs to use.

We have found that the idea of personal lexicon is very attractive to students. They like thinking that their brains come with their own libraries, dictionaries, and thesauruses that are discerned from studying, prior learning, interests, and current themes. Knowing this allows us to underscore and reiterate their uniqueness.

Using student drawings based on their understanding of text assures that they "got" the lesson.

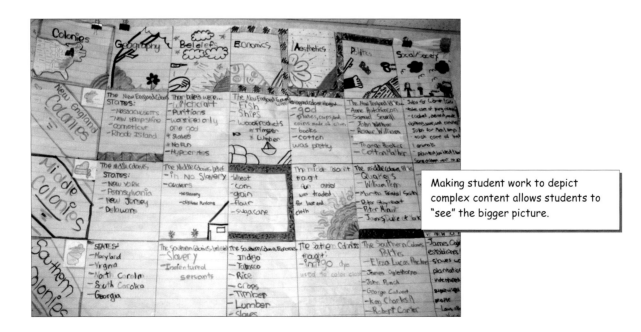

Making student work to depict complex content allows students to "see" the bigger picture.

The Literate Environment: Vocabulary and Content

"Given that students' success in school and beyond depends in great measure upon their ability to read with comprehension, there is urgency to providing instruction that equips students with the skills and strategies necessary for lifelong vocabulary development."

Fran Lehr, M.A., Jean Osborn, M.Ed.,
Dr. Elfrieda H. Hiebert

According to Louisa Moats, one of the leading vocabulary gurus, the gap in word knowledge between advantaged and disadvantaged children is called "word poverty" and is exacerbated every year that the student lives without a rich literate environment and "robust vocabulary" (Beck). As educators, one of the best campaigns we can take on is one that involves reading, vocabulary, or comprehension. We prefer the vocabulary efforts. Other colleagues target reading to get to vocabulary and comprehension. Our preference is getting to reading and comprehension through the vocabulary door.

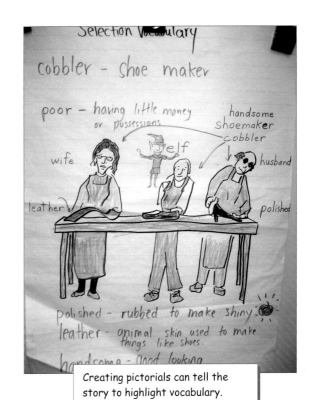

Creating pictorials can tell the story to highlight vocabulary.

Providing children with opportunities to fully engage in the learning experience makes understanding easier and more fun!

The Literate Environment: Vocabulary and Content

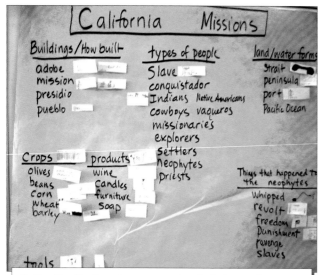

Reflecting the learning process visually helps students remember. Here, the students sorted the words for the study of missions around categories that made sense to them and then illustrated the words quickly with Post-its. This activity was done as a review using the textbook. The students determined the categories and then located the words as they reviewed the textbook chapter. They displayed these words on individual white boards for sharing, then the teacher scribed their selections for them into categories.

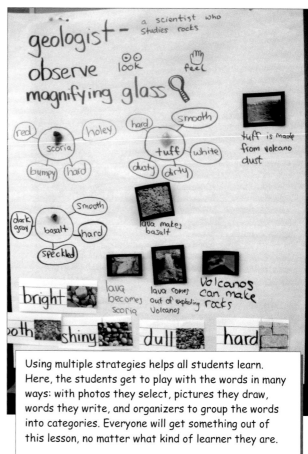

Using multiple strategies helps all students learn. Here, the students get to play with the words in many ways: with photos they select, pictures they draw, words they write, and organizers to group the words into categories. Everyone will get something out of this lesson, no matter what kind of learner they are.

Teaching vocabulary means playing with words in lots of ways. Word sorts are an important vocabulary tool for matching definitions and activities.

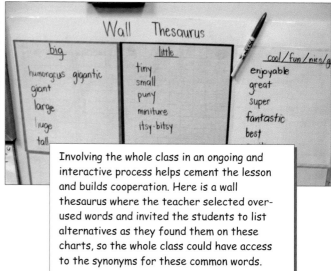

Involving the whole class in an ongoing and interactive process helps cement the lesson and builds cooperation. Here is a wall thesaurus where the teacher selected over-used words and invited the students to list alternatives as they found them on these charts, so the whole class could have access to the synonyms for these common words.

The Literate Environment: Vocabulary and Content

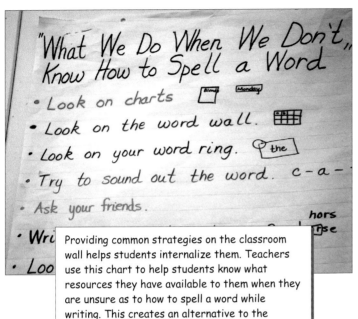

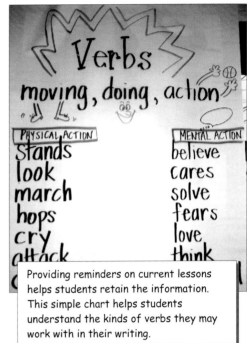

> Providing common strategies on the classroom wall helps students internalize them. Teachers use this chart to help students know what resources they have available to them when they are unsure as to how to spell a word while writing. This creates an alternative to the question, "Teacher, can you spell…?"

> Providing reminders on current lessons helps students retain the information. This simple chart helps students understand the kinds of verbs they may work with in their writing.

Tiered Vocabulary Multiple Meanings

1 EVERYBODY	II EDUCATED PEOPLE	III EXPERTS	
make	build	architect:	erects
	create	scientist:	invents
	type	car salesman:	style
	earn	parents:	acquire
	bring about	lawyer:	cause
good	kind	teacher:	thoughtful, considerate
	able	carpenter:	expert
	interesting	movie goer:	thrilling
	polite	parents:	well-behaved, well-mannered
	fine	antique dealer:	perfect, undamaged
break	crack	nurse/doctor:	fracture
	pause, rest	movie goer:	intermission
	not follow	parents:	disobey
clear	see-through	artist:	transparent
	simple	writer:	uncomplicated, straight-forward

Tiered Vocabulary

1 EVERYBODY	II EDUCATED PEOPLE	III EXPERTS:	
do	able	employee:	competent
above	upper	snob:	utmost
across	crossways	police:	intersection
scared	afraid	Wizard of Oz:	cowardly
past	ago	teacher:	history
in front	ahead	clerk:	forward
air	breeze	scientist:	atmosphere
just about	almost	teacher:	nearly
always	constantly	doctor:	regularly
mad	angry	actor:	livid
answer	reply, solve	scientist:	solution
anyone	anybody	teacher	whomever
anything	any item	kids' slang:	whatever
house	apartment	realtor:	condominium
arm	limb	doctor:	extremity
sleeping	asleep	zoologist:	dormant, hibernate

> Demonstrating formal and casual register is an important aspect of teaching vocabulary. Tiering vocabulary is one of the language development tasks that the students really enjoy. It introduces the concepts of casual and formal register, and the idea of code switching – being able to choose which speech vernacular that you can use based on your audience. Tiered vocabulary is a wonderful way to explode language. If you really want to "kick it up a notch," have the students make an ICON – a symbol for each word,
> *(There is a blank chart in the Tool Kit on page 126.)*

The Literate Environment: Collaborative Writing

Writing is a complex problem-solving process. Students need to not only figure out how to come up with ideas, organize their thoughts, and select words to express them, but how to handle all of the mechanics of writing as well. Collaborative or shared writing frees up students to focus on their ideas and content, while the teacher manages the conventions of spelling, grammar, punctuation, and format.

During collaborative writing the teacher orchestrates the contributions of all of the students creating the piece. Techniques such as heads together, individual white boards, or brainstorming on a piece of chart paper assure that all of the voices are heard before the ideas to include in the piece are written down. If a student offers an idea for a sentence that is spoken with incorrect grammar, the teacher can gently suggest another way to say the same thing in standard English. Before the teacher writes a sentence down, the whole class "rehearses" the sentence orally to listen for sense and flow.

Teachers who regularly write with their whole class and post those pieces as models for thinking and writing build a sense of community. These classrooms are filled with texts that all students can read and recall because they wrote them themselves.

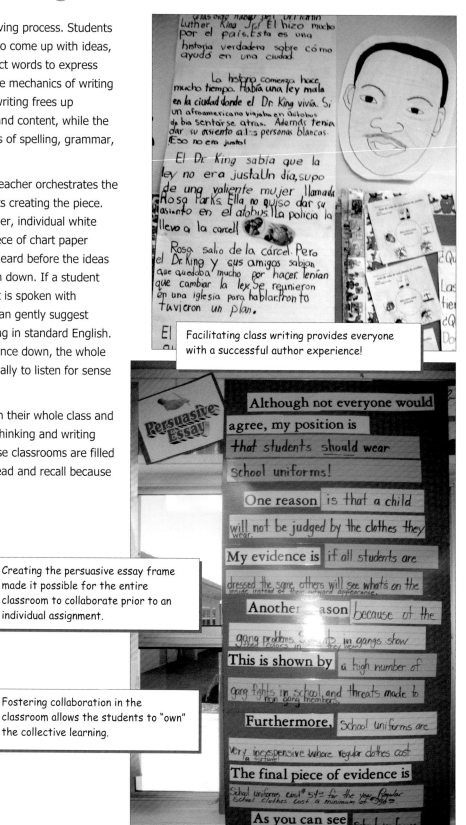

Facilitating class writing provides everyone with a successful author experience!

Creating the persuasive essay frame made it possible for the entire classroom to collaborate prior to an individual assignment.

Fostering collaboration in the classroom allows the students to "own" the collective learning.

The Literate Environment:
Collaborative Writing

Collaborating in a fifth grade persuasive writing project will result in a more convincing individual assignment.

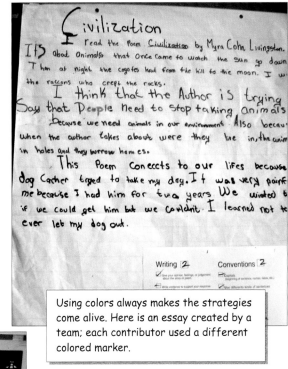

Using colors always makes the strategies come alive. Here is an essay created by a team; each contributor used a different colored marker.

Providing publishing opportunities improves writing morale.

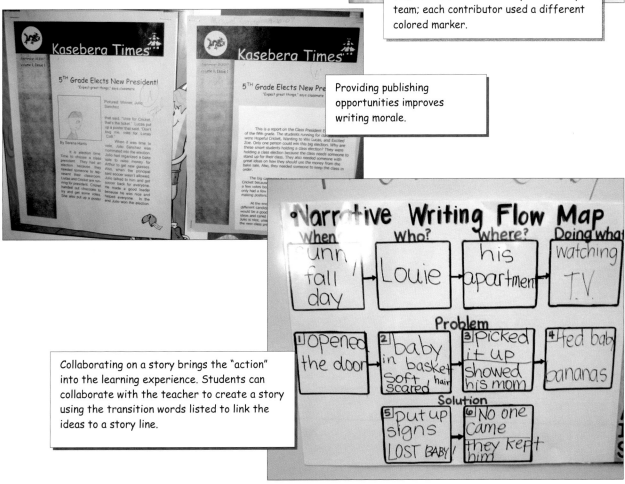

Collaborating on a story brings the "action" into the learning experience. Students can collaborate with the teacher to create a story using the transition words listed to link the ideas to a story line.

The Literate Environment: Writing Portfolio Walls

Writing is one way to create evidence of improvement and validate effort and hard work. Most students are unclear how about the relationship between work/effort/trying and outcomes. Ask a student how they got an "A" and most will tell you they don't know. Some will even report that perhaps the teacher was in a good mood.

We recommend the use of rubrics and frequent feedback. Students need to understand what they are doing right so that they can replicate the effort to duplicate the outcome. You have to ask yourself, "Is this feedback going to help my student understand what is good about this paper? Will she be able to do it again on the next paper?" The rubric describes the expectations for each level of performance.

A writing portfolio wall gives students the space to display a current piece of published writing for all to see. Over the course of a year, students will see the writing development of the whole class grow as they read each other's pieces each month. If you use plastic sheet protectors, a clipboard, or brads and clips to mount the writing, students can leave each monthly piece in a collection posted all year long. Parents and teachers can lift the pieces and see how writing has developed over time. Alternatively, teachers can take down the published writing each month and bind it into a class anthology for each project. These can be circulated in the school library or within the classroom grade level.

Connecting big ideas prepares students to write.

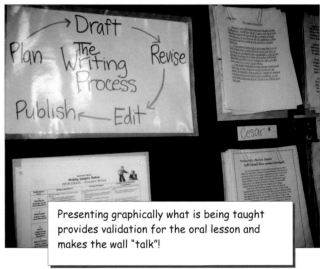

Presenting graphically what is being taught provides validation for the oral lesson and makes the wall "talk"!

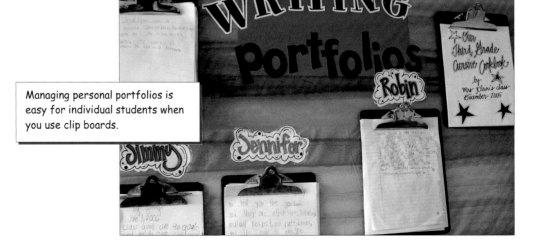

Managing personal portfolios is easy for individual students when you use clip boards.

The Literate Environment: Writing Portfolio Walls

Post the writing standards, rubric, and any other needed information for the current writing being displayed on the same wall. Teachers and students can add comments to highlight the content of the posted writing in several ways: Post-it notes with comments, mini checklists attached to the writing, more formal rubric scoring attached.

Students will take particular pride in displaying their work if each section is decorated with a photo of the student, the student name typed or posted in bold print, and a colorful mat to show off the writing. When appropriate, have students illustrate their writing with original art work.

Displaying student work is always tricky. Present the work that meets or exceeds the rubric for proficiency. It is also possible to post work that does something extremely well – best topic sentence or closure. Try to display all students' work at some time during the students' life in your classroom. Do it in a manner that the students' efforts garner applause from their peers at the grade level. **Never post something you know will cause trouble or embarrassment for a student**.

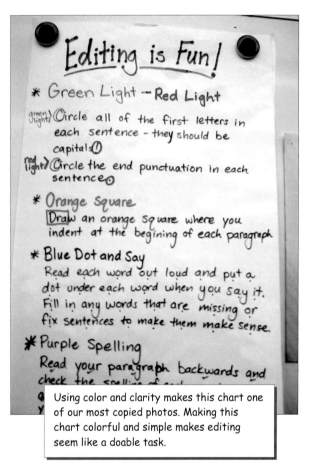

Using color and clarity makes this chart one of our most copied photos. Making this chart colorful and simple makes editing seem like a doable task.

Keeping it simple has made writing and its mechanics easy to do when using this teacher-made chart.

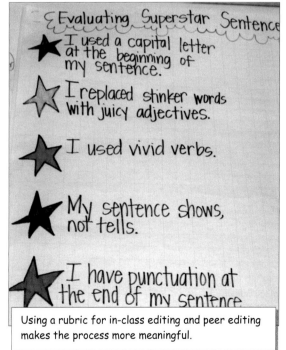

Using a rubric for in-class editing and peer editing makes the process more meaningful.

The Literate Environment: Writing Portfolio Walls

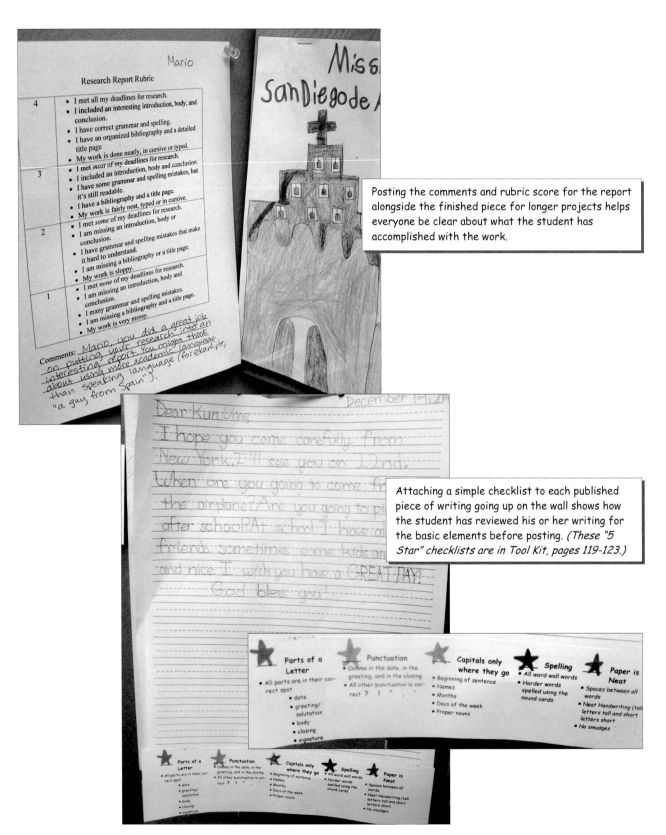

Posting the comments and rubric score for the report alongside the finished piece for longer projects helps everyone be clear about what the student has accomplished with the work.

Attaching a simple checklist to each published piece of writing going up on the wall shows how the student has reviewed his or her writing for the basic elements before posting. (These "5 Star" checklists are in Tool Kit, pages 119-123.)

The Literate Environment: Writing Portfolio Walls

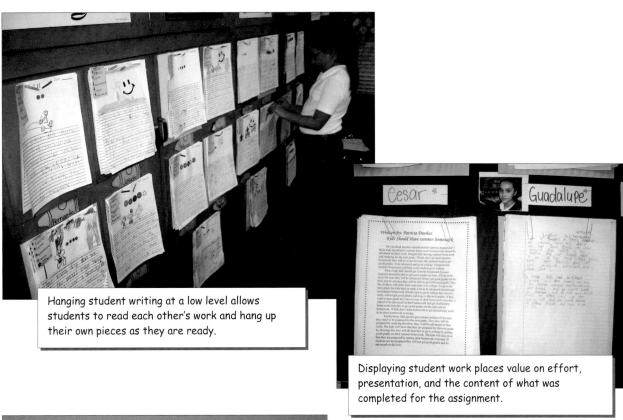

Hanging student writing at a low level allows students to read each other's work and hang up their own pieces as they are ready.

Displaying student work places value on effort, presentation, and the content of what was completed for the assignment.

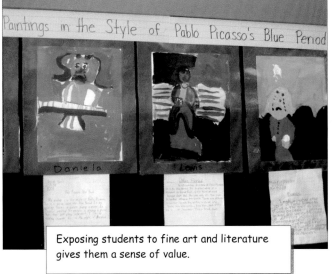

Exposing students to fine art and literature gives them a sense of value.

Seeing your work and the work of others is validating, exciting, and fun!

Standards & Targets

The No Child Left Behind Act of 2001 called for increased national accountability and improved student achievement in language arts and math. At the heart of this improved achievement is the curriculum — the "road map" that ensures that every student receives instruction based on state standards and outcomes. According to Swain and Pearson (2002), "A standards-based curriculum will level the playing field for all students" (T.H.E. Journal, May 2003).

We utilized the California State Standards throughout *Talking Walls.* They exist as our yardstick for all lessons and assessments. We recommend that the standards being taught need to be displayed and referred to directly during the lesson. Students need to understand that these are the grade-level norms and the goal is to meet or exceed them.

Students and parents are alerted to the standards being taught during the course of the year at the beginning of school and during parent-teacher conferences. During instruction, students are also made aware of the standards on which they will be tested and how the current lesson relates to those assessments.

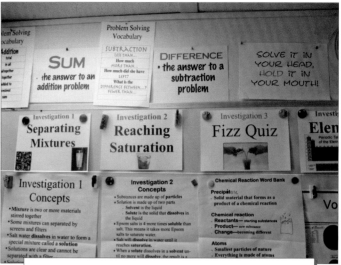

Defining terms and making the complex comprehensible helps students understand the content.

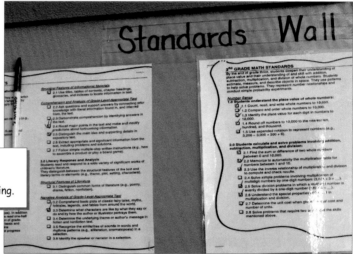

Checking off standards as they are delivered, studied, or mastered lets students know what they are accomplishing.

Organizing weekly targets from grade-level standards keeps students informed of instructional objectives.

Standards & Targets

The lesson objectives are planned ahead of time. The specific standards to be addressed are included in the lesson plan, along with an expected outcome and an assessment to determine the success of instructional delivery. The standards are the architecture upon which lessons rely. BUT, the teacher's creativity and relationship with the student are what make the standards make sense. Meaning is derived from the experiences in the classroom.

Checking standards can become a meaningful aspect of student work.

Managing simple public recognition displays such as this one can be very motivating for skills that require rote memorization. In this case, students earn their name on a star each time they master a new set of math facts.

Honing the standards with student-created materials embeds learning by making it real.

Standards & Targets

Assessments include a variety of procedures to gather information about what the students know and don't know, and what they can and cannot do. These assessments and the data gleaned from them are used to guide instruction.

Targets and standards serve a number of discrete functions within the classroom:

1. Let students know what is important to learn

2. Provide information to students and parents about student progress

3. Help students learn to evaluate their own learning

4. Improve instruction by determining targets

5. Identify students that need extra services or intervention.

"Classroom assessment remains the most important direct influence on students' day-to-day learning" (Project 2011).

Simplifying terms helps everyone stay focused. The vocabulary needs to be comprehensible and experienced in real-world tasks. Assessments should help the students understand what they need to know.

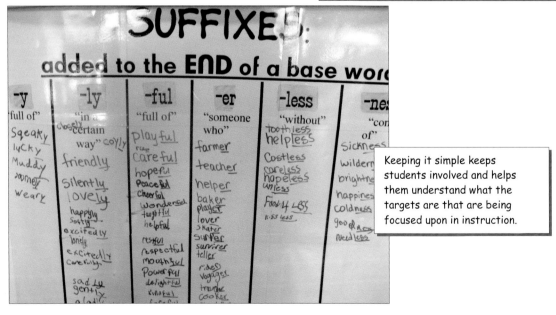

Keeping it simple keeps students involved and helps them understand what the targets are that are being focused upon in instruction.

Standards & Targets

The more students are actively engaged in the development of their course work and the artifacts the more tangible their learning.

Students need to meet high standards in a context that has meaning and relevance in their everyday lives.

The grade-level standards and the content standards provide norms for learning. The goal is to exceed the norm. Students need to understand that going beyond the standard is the greater challenge of achievement.

The instructional targets need to be prominently displayed to underscore their importance and value to the current standard.

We have standards for learning but not standard learners. We do not want to encourage a one-size-fits all type of environment or classroom presentation. Instead, the classroom needs to validate that all students can learn to high standards and meet high expectations.

STANDARDS OVERVIEW for the WEEK of _____

READING/LANGUAGE ARTS

Word Analysis:_____

Reading Comprehension:_____

Literary Analysis:_____

Written Conventions:_____

Writing Strategies:_____

Writing Applications:_____

MATHEMATICS

Number Sense 1 & 2:_____

Number Sense 3 & 4:_____

Algebra & Functions:_____

Measurement & Geometry:_____

Statistics:_____

We've included the Standards Overview for the Week in the Tool Kit and on the CD.

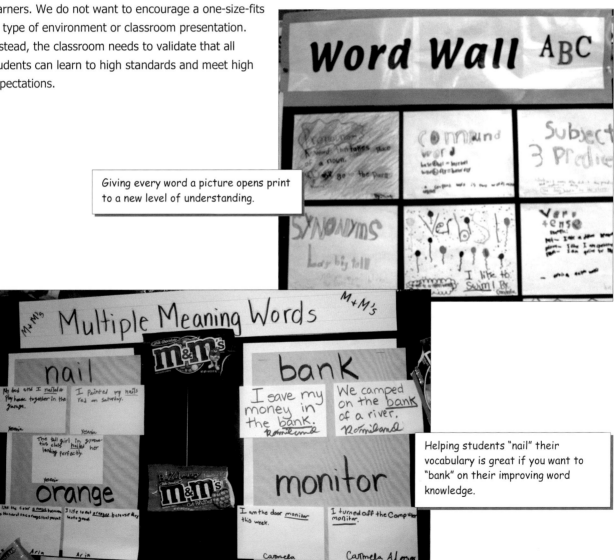

Giving every word a picture opens print to a new level of understanding.

Helping students "nail" their vocabulary is great if you want to "bank" on their improving word knowledge.

Feedback & Data: Progress Monitoring

Progress-monitoring is one of the most important tools for a school in reform. It will help inform a teacher's decisions for planning ahead or for the instructional day at hand. It asks the teacher to consider what is next and also provides a context to easily identify what is missing. For parents, progress-monitoring provides the concrete evidence of a student's efforts at school. If a parent asks, "How is my child doing in math?" or, "How are his language arts skills?" there is not only a way to express this clearly, but also a model that encourages this type of communication between student, parent, and teacher.

A student wants to know where he or she stands. The question often is, "What do I know?" or "What do I need to know?" Most students will enjoy a sense of accomplishment when they see their scores improve. A caring teacher can help engender achievement and mitigate barriers to learning using these tools.

There may be a differentiated set of criteria for some students. For example, the student may only be required to complete 10 of 15 problems for a homework assignment. There is no changing of grade-level status or standard. Instead, it is the workload or time allotted that might be changed. These criteria might be determined by the Individual Educational Plan (IEP) or an intervention action plan orchestrated by a Student Study Team.

A creative display allows students to see the benefit of their hard work.

Looking at data need not mean capturing student progress in numbers — using metaphors works well too. Sometimes ducks or "smarty pants" tell the story better.

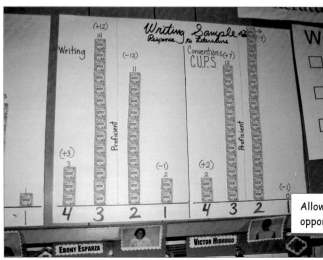

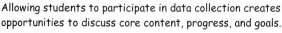

Allowing students to participate in data collection creates opportunities to discuss core content, progress, and goals.

Feedback & Data: Displaying Student Data

Data is the symbolic representation of an outcome. It has no value until it is attached to something that has meaning. Connect data to something that is important to the group and then draw the group into the act of data analysis. In this way you can transform a relatively dry thought process into an engaging group activity.

We need to use data at school to tell stories of student achievement, teacher efficacy, institutional success, and parent involvement. The strength-based paradigm is an investment in the future. Prosocial models offer concrete feedback about what is working and what can be improved. They manifest success and utilize the "pedagogy of no regrets" (Dennis Parker, 2005).

These photos depict a montage of ways that teachers have shown student data. Note that there is no single correct approach. Make the process a learning experience and have the students vote on the type of graph they want to represent their formative data. One teacher used her sixth-grade student council to make the decision. They opted to use their first names and actual scores. Interestingly, the California Standards Test scores indicated that 100% of the students were proficient in math. Student involvement in the monitoring and acquisition of grade-level standards seems to accelerate their progress and achievement.

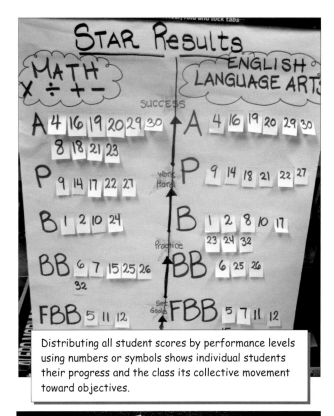

Distributing all student scores by performance levels using numbers or symbols shows individual students their progress and the class its collective movement toward objectives.

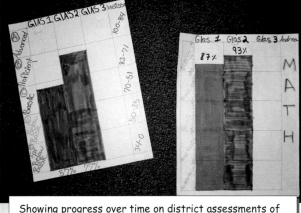

Showing progress over time on district assessments of English language arts and math, one student has mapped her progress. As you can see, she has improved her score from one test to the next.

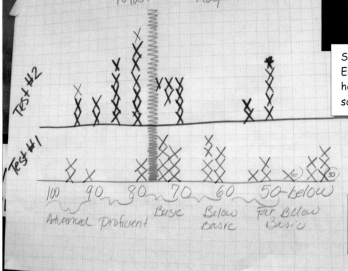

Collapsing data into specific chunks can give immediate feedback to students about their performance.

Feedback & Data: Evidence of Engagement

The students who work well in teams need the validation of seeing their work posted on the wall and acknowledged by their peers and other adults. They also enjoy praise and validation from professionals who are often invited to class. Negative behavior seems to be lessened and prosocial behavior increases when students see that their input is appreciated and that they have a valued place in the classroom.

Prosocial engagement has three discrete elements:

1. a meaningful topic;

2. demeanor of presenters; and

3. success-oriented future focus

Each of these elements require that the students participate to the best of their ability.

Enabling students to create the curriculum is possible with facilitation!

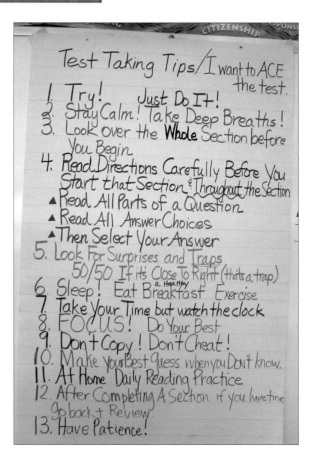

Feedback & Data: Collective Engagement

Students enjoy competition when everyone gets involved and the rules are fair. With differentiation and teaching the students caring responsibility, there should be no problem allowing all students the time to "grow" into successful classroom participants.

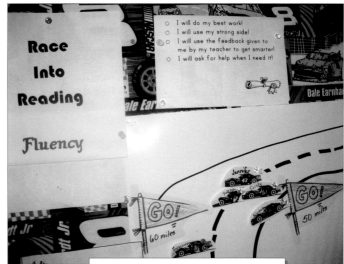

Creating metaphors sometimes provides the excitement needed for a campaign.

Representing success by name should be agreed upon prior to posting. Agreeing to the rules of participation assures that more effort will be generated!

Giving every child a goal in a collective process is inclusion at its best.

Feedback & Data: Collective Engagement

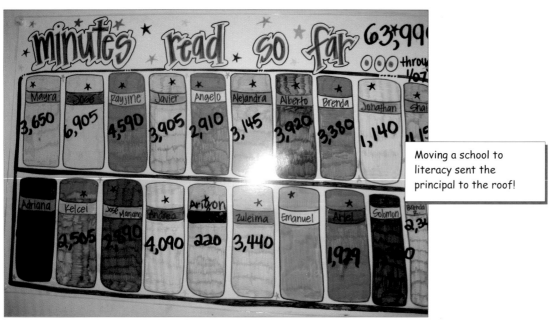

Moving a school to literacy sent the principal to the roof!

Growing success occurs with every public posting of goal attainment.

Coordinating campaigns often engage students in reading better than any other motivator. All member students love to have the principal do weird things: kiss a pig, send out on the roof, wear a dress (male), or shave his or her head!

Feedback & Data: Collective Engagement

Each of these pictures is evidence that the students are actively and purposely involved in a real-time instructional objective. Not only do they come to school, they monitor their own progress and their peers' achievement, and follow their own learning plan. This plan reflects the levels of responsibility students can embrace, given the opportunity.

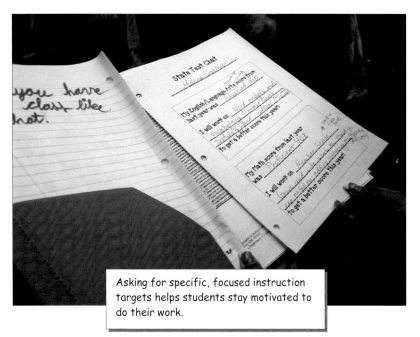

Asking for specific, focused instruction targets helps students stay motivated to do their work.

Providing opportunities for students to monitor their own effort promotes "personal best" competition and self-monitoring.

Feedback & Data: Progress Campaigns

One of the most effective ways to focus students on particular targets is to help them organize their own campaigns. When students invest in the process of a campaign, they develop the skills and behaviors needed to change their world. This is called social marketing.

Students who are engaged in active campaigns chart their progress, enjoy celebrations of their success, and see evidence of achievement in their learning environment. They are more likely to stay hooked on school and connected to their future. They are taking a stand for themselves and their learning community.

How does this work? We ask students to care about each other and invest in one another's success. Helping others without asking for something in return, sharing materials, offering support or advice, working in teams, and thinking together all prepare our students for the improvement of self. Campaigns shape expected behavior, and the creativity of students is what makes it work.

Posting a student's writing on her door allows the teacher to provide feedback and encouragement – instantly!

Revealing test scores and competing for progress on the CST can be made fun, motivating, and encouraging with student-produced art and banners.

Meta-cognition

"He who learns but does not think is lost."

— Chinese Proverb

Teaching students how to think can be compared to the old adage: "Give a man a fish; you have fed him for today. Teach a man to fish; and you have fed him for a lifetime." The same is true of learning. We can teach discrete skills. The student will know how to do that one thing but may not know how to connect that skill to prior learning. This is called learning in isolation.

Many children describe this process in terms that indicate their perception that teachers are "doing something to them" to make them learn. They'll say, "She makes us." "She told us." "He said we had to." "He won't let us."

Facilitating the academic language of meta-cognition allows children to think and say it congruently.

We believe that students need to be metacognitively engaged. That is, they should constantly reflect on their thinking and how it connects to their previous learning, and what they need to know. To do this well, the teachers and the other students become apt at inquiry and the ensuing dialogues that are brought forth from deep questioning. The New Bloom's Taxonomy, authored in 2001 by Bloom and his associates, makes teaching students how to question at varying levels of cognition possible. Bloom also sets students up to be personally reflective by looking at levels of cognition in terms of personal applications, evaluations, and opinions.

(See Bloom's Taxonomy prompts and work sheets in the Tool Kit, pages 137-143, and on the CD.)

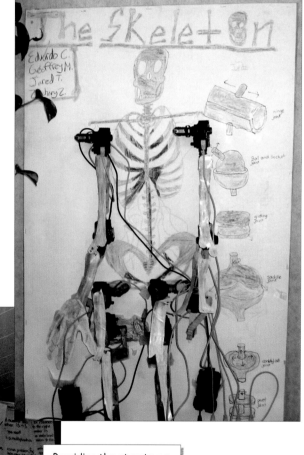

Providing the structures for learning gives students a way to understand both process and content.

Meta-cognition: New Bloom's Taxonomy

Bloom's Taxonomy is an effective tool to teach students how to question and develop thinking skills. These skills are integral to the development of metacognition and a rigorous understanding of content or tactics that will lead to mastery. We developed a color-coded student prompt aligned with Bloom's Taxonomy to teach questioning techniques *(see the Toolkit)*. For example, after teaching a concept or reading a story, the teacher might say, "Give me a yellow question regarding the story." (REMEMBER: yellow), or "How did you perceive her strengths?" (EVALUATE: green). "What kind of a question is that?"

Teaching the taxonomy to students using the terms described at each level is difficult without a visual prompt. We have been very successful using the color-coded process and linking the verbs to the level of cognition. By using the colors and the verbs, the students seem to develop an understanding of the questioning process before they tackle the level of inquiry required for the assignment.

(See Bloom's Taxonomy prompts and worksheets in the Tool Kit, pages 137-143, and on the CD.)

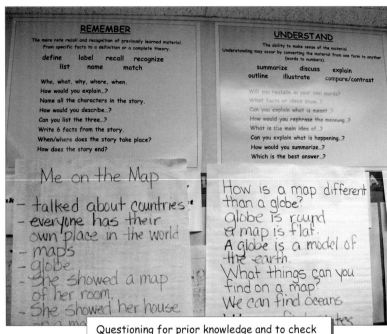

Questioning for prior knowledge and to check for understanding allows students to benefit from one another's experience and thinking.

Helping students to learn to think and question is paramount to their later success in school and in life.

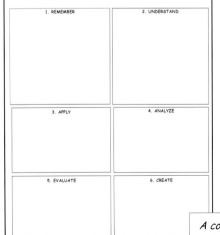

A copy of this Bloom's Taxonomy Student Work Sheet is in the Tool Kit on page 143 on the CD.

Connecting to the Future

The resiliency literature describes characteristics that mitigate and protect young people from stress and chaos. One of the most potent protective factors is having a future-focused plan. This plan helps students go outside of their current circumstances and forecast another reality in which they have control. Taking personal control helps many students follow through on a plan that many might view impossible. Education makes the impossible possible.

Education relies on students believing in a future. Studying is investing in the future. Planning for a career or a degree is all about a future event.

Students have to *see* themselves wearing the white coat of the veterinarian, or the special jacket of an executive chef working at the White House cooking for the president. "I just kept seeing myself walking across the stage to get my degree and that's how I keep going. No matter what happens. I stay focused on that stage!" said one recent graduate.

Wayne Gretzky, the hockey player, said his success was from the fact that he "skated to where the puck was going to be." He won because he played into the future!

Taking students to the future requires that they step into the possibilities of what they can become.

Helping students see themselves in the future as capable and competent college students is a challenge and the gift education offers every child.

Connecting to the Future

When students start to understand what it takes to go to college and a get four-year degree, many of them decide to become more engaged in school. Others question whether or not they have the capacity to make it. It is important to show young people that all kinds of students make it in college. Career goal-setting is not a one-size-fits-all process. It is about the *choices* students make in light of their interests and experiences, and how their worldview is based on what they have learned and want to learn.

Making choices starts with having choices to make. For example, in many California middle schools, the only students who have choices for electives are those who have passed math and language arts at a proficient level. Below proficiency, the students have to enroll in courses that are supportive of language arts or math, which gives them a double dose of the core curriculum, but no choices.

To have choices in school, the typical student has to demonstrate the capacity to meet the standards in the basic requirements. From this position, they can start to connect to the future through educational coursework.

Personal control in their lives can be enhanced when they have choices.

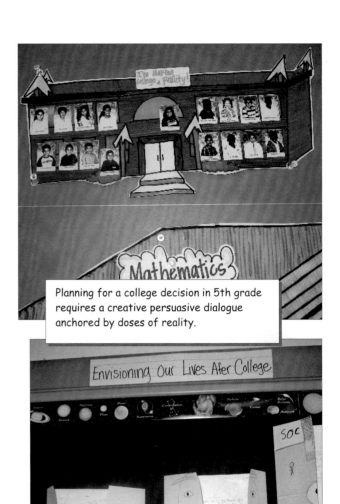

Planning for a college decision in 5th grade requires a creative persuasive dialogue anchored by doses of reality.

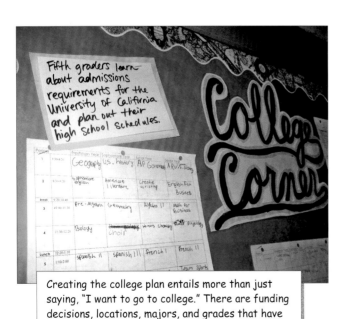

Creating the college plan entails more than just saying, "I want to go to college." There are funding decisions, locations, majors, and grades that have to be considered. Letters of recommendation from teachers have to be written!

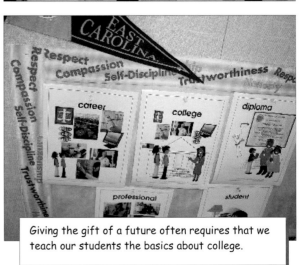

Giving the gift of a future often requires that we teach our students the basics about college.

Portrait of a Middle School Classroom

What every middle school needs is a faculty full of student motivators. Middle schools all over the United States are having a hard time embracing the challenges of reform. They are the slowest schools to get out of Program Improvement (PI) and the least likely to help students move out of lower performance strands. There is an increasing population of youth dropping out of school in the eighth grade!

The research is very clear—many adolescent males determine how school is going to fit into their future based on what happens in their intermediate and middle school experiences. Adolescent girls sometimes get so distracted by social and emotional issues in the intermediate and middle grades they never get back on the academic track. The more disconnected students are from positive feedback regarding their academic performance the less likely it is that the youth will push themselves to do the hard work required in grades 4 through 8.

The teacher of young adolescents has to be one part comic, one part counselor, and one part content expert. They have to create the conditions in which the students can learn through high interest learning activities. The best of these teachers are both great communicators and phenomenally intuitive. They are attractive people. Not physically attractive—although that does not hurt—necessarily, but appealing to youth. The attraction happens with humor, stability and organization, knowing the subject, how to give feedback, and a myriad of strategies that would only look good on you. From this attraction, rapport is built, and with *rapport* permission is generated to ask questions, touch, or even require high expectations. These are the characteristics of influence which is the foundation of the teacher-student relationship that leads to empowerment.

Empowerment is the essence of independent learning and the management of personal curiosity. The ultimate goal is to help a student reach for the reality of autopoiesis, which is how we invent ourselves through learning—we literally self-produce through how we target our education. That is why we declare majors in college—they want to know how we plan on becoming.

During the course of creating this book, we ran into a number of teachers who had the capacity to help students invent themselves. These teachers communicated well with youth, they are both intuitively and technically skilled, their instruction is memorable and meaningful, the classroom culture was non-threatening and prosocial, and above all, the students learn as was evidenced by assessment. These teachers are not publicly declaring themselves masters of the classroom nor are they communicating that they are doing it right while others are wrong. They are dedicated and focused folks with students on the mind.

We ran into two such folks who impressed us so much that we decided to feature their classrooms. We call them **The Middle School Motivators**. Teaching students who are 80% free or reduced lunch, Maureen Ferry and Kilian Betlach promote significant academic gains with the majority of their students, moving over 70% to proficient.

Portrait of a Middle School Classroom

We think their stories hint at what it takes to create a teaching workforce that can answer the needs of the urban poor. The first impression when we met the dynamic duo was their energy—even though we were meeting a few days after school closed, both Maureen and Kilian were quite animated and excited to talk about their students and their classrooms. They used current literature to describe what worked and did not work in their day to day operations. They had quite a story to tell about how they came to this place in their career. It seems that they were both enticed by Teach for America (TFA) through a recruitment process at their university. That is what got them to the classroom; the students and the exhilaration of success kept them there. It would be good to know more about them.

Kilian Betlach

There were nearly 15,000 applicants for only 2,000 possible positions the year that Kilian was accepted into TFA. He had no idea of the rigor and demands that teaching in a high need classroom had in store for him. He was pleased to secure a position and pleased that he had somehow competed successfully. He was told that he was selected because he was smart, ambitious, and curious. He found that he would need each of these skills during his two year commitment. The TFA process involved intensive training and an ongoing relationship with a cohort of other trainees. However, it was the relationship with the colleagues on staff at his school that contributed to the collective efficacy experienced by the school. They worked hard together to make their classrooms and the school work well. The administrator was an effective leader and supported his teachers. Kilian was curious and wanted to know how to do the best job possible, he was smart and could assimilate information quickly, but most of all he was ambitious. Kilian was going to take his students where no TFA teacher had ever gone before: 3 in 1! He expected three years growth in one year. The students bought into the goal and together they set out to achieve it. While challenging students in the classroom on a daily basis, Kilian found time to complete his MA at San Jose State.

After graduating from Boston College with a B.A. in Psychology, Philosophy, and American Studies in 2002, Kilian decided to channel his passions for Literature and Social Change into teaching for two years as a Teach for America Corps Member. At a middle school in East San Jose, CA, Kilian's TFA placement school, he quickly became known as the young, fiery, teacher with exceedingly high expectations and a vision for student success and school reform. In his second year, Kilian began teaching English Language Arts to Below Basic and Far Below Basic seventh graders, most of whom were English language learners and had experienced little success prior to their year in Mr. Betlach's class. At the start of the year, Kilian hoped to lead his students, some of whom did not know the alphabet, to 1.5 years of growth in ELA; however, after assessing mid-year, he realized his students were far exceeding his original projections. He then developed a theme, "3-in-1," because he knew that in order for his students to advance near grade level, three years of growth in one year were necessary. More importantly, it was possible.

Outside of the classroom, alongside an effective and visionary principal and some dedicated teachers, Kilian contributed instrumentally to the reform that brought the school from the lowest performing school in the district to the highest in four years. He also set a high standard for the 12 additional TFA teachers to teach at the school in the coming years.

Portrait of a Middle School Classroom

Maureen Ferry

Maureen came to the TFA experience because she believed in the mission and felt it provided an opportunity to apply her skills in the service of social justice. She was placed at the middle school where Kilian and eight other TFA teachers were already in place. It was a unique staff. By the start of the next school year, nearly half the staff would be comprised of TFA teachers, many of whom had already completed their two-year commitment and chose to continue teaching. It was unusual to say the least. Maureen was younger than her colleagues but just as dedicated and energetic. Through trial by fire, she developed her own repertoire of skills and interventions. Soon she became one of the teachers "in the know". Her benchmark scores rose dramatically and behavior problems were reduced. Her CST assessment in her second year of teaching indicated that over 80% of her students were proficient in math.

Maureen Ferry graduated from the University of Michigan in 2005 with a bachelor's degree in Economics and Psychology. She was accepted into Teach for America and became a 7th/8th grade math and algebra teacher. In her first year, Maureen was assigned a core of the most at-risk 7th graders, a vote of confidence in her abilities typically reserved for more experienced educators. Encountering substantial difficulties, Maureen worked relentlessly to bring change to her classes. She wrote continuous personal reflections on teaching and management, collaborated with colleagues on ways to communicate appreciation and provide positive feedback to her students, and simply dug in, refusing to give in or lower her expectations. The work paid off. Maureen's classroom excellence is typified by her class theme, "Are you on the college track?"—a constant reminder of the ambition and purpose underlying all teaching and learning. Maureen extended these expectations outside of her classroom, convincing the school administration to increase the number of students enrolled in algebra by fifty percent, and choosing to provide algebra instruction to students typically denied access to such critical content. Maureen enrolled and completed her master's degree during this time!

Maureen's work is characterized by high expectations, rigorous structure, and an unyielding focus on student achievement. Yet, it is the quality of relationships that set her apart as an exemplary educator. As cross-country coach and founder of the school's first dance team, she connects with a wide array of students, building positive school experiences. Her classroom is a widely acknowledged as a special place, filled with celebrations of student success, such as the "100 club" for perfect performance on assessments and the "Are you tough enough?" awards for strong in-class work. Her classroom is a place of warmth and welcome where students can be found congregating before and after school. It is a place where the lasting rapport she builds with students is as valuable and rare as the tremendous academic gains they achieve together. At 80% proficient, her students have exceeded site, district, state and national norms. Maureen has accepted a new position at a KIPP school in San Francisco for the 2008-2009 school year.

Portrait of a Middle School Classroom

We wanted to check our understanding of how Maureen and Kilian organized and operated in the classroom. We posed the following questions for your benefit. Hopefully you will find them as enlightening as we did.

An Interview with Maureen and Kilian: The Middle School Motivators

1. **Our book is called *Talking Walls*, is this appropriate descriptor of what happens in your classroom? Tell us why or why not.**

Maureen:	*Kilian:*
On a daily basis I refer to the walls for a past problem or to check on a formula or a mnemonic device. My students like seeing their work on the walls and like seeing utility in future lessons. It always amazes me how excited students are to have their work selected for display.	Of course the use of space is critical, and I want to display things on my walls that reflect what is important and critical in my classroom. In that sense, my walls *talk* – to kids, families, visitors – what I'm about as a teacher, and what type of environment we will create in my classroom.

2. **What are the most important things that you display prominently on your walls?**

Maureen:	*Kilian:*
Student work is the most important presentation in the classroom. I like to show exemplary work and models for examples of difficult concepts. My students like to see that math is real and can be applied to everyday life. I always find a way to legitimize and validate everyone's paper turned in.	First, the **3-in-1** posters. There are four of these, and one is hung directly over the door. It's the first thing you see, this poster you need to pass under to enter the room, because it exists as the first principle of the work we do together. In direct line of sight from the door are the four Big Goals posters, which outline the specific academic benchmarks all students will reach. I hang additional posters that are connected to content objectives, past and present. These exist as reference points and contribute to a print-rich environment that is critical for English language learners.

Portrait of a Middle School Classroom

An Interview with Maureen and Killian: The Middle School Motivators

3. **What kinds of student works are posted? Do you ever display work that is not at grade level?**

Maureen:	*Kilian:*
I don't post work with errors. I think that is the nature of math. There is no real draft-rewrite stage. Displaying math is really a celebration and demonstration of correct usage.	I primarily display student work connected to our reading comprehension/ analysis work. These include graphic organizers for specific reading strategies, formal written responses, and mini-projects that demonstrate understanding and application of key concepts. I have not taught a student that began the year at grade level since 2002, so of course I display work that is below what is considered proficient. I try to prevent certain students from dominating the selection of displayed work, but at the same time, I do not want to lower standards. Displaying work is not the only method of praise and recognition available to students, but it is one in which I recognize ultimate achievement rather than incremental growth.

4. **What value do you perceive that illustrations, doodles, icons or drawings have in every day efforts?**

Maureen:	*Kilian:*
Visualizing or "seeing" in math makes the work real. It is a key strategy. The most successful math students can "see" the order of operation and it helps them make sense out of how to answer the questions.	I've had a lot of great student-artists, and I try to provide space for those skills, both formally and informally. In terms of walls, I try to provide space—typically behind my desk—for kids to display their own, non-academic artistic endeavors.

Portrait of a Middle School Classroom

An Interview with Maureen and Kilian: The Middle School Motivators

5. **Do you use data walls? Who maintains them? What data is used and do the students know who is succeeding and who is falling behind? How do you manage the crisis of failure?**

Maureen:	*Kilian:*
I like data walls when we are monitoring a specific target or competing with another class. They are very useful prior to testing, during test chats with students, and as a way to talk about the performance of the class.	I've transported the data walls into progress tracking folders. Students maintain numerous progress monitoring charts covering everything from fluency to writing to acquisition of reading strategies. Data generally come from a wide variety of assessments, and is generally presented to students in as clear a manner as possible. For example, when updating Big Goal #3 sheets (improve independent reading level 2.0 grade levels) students will receive a slip of paper with their fluency scores for both fiction and non-fiction, and update accordingly. I mediate the "falling behindness" in two ways: 1) by providing ample opportunities for reteaching and reassessing; and 2) by creating goals that measure growth, rather than attainment of a fixed end point, allowing kids who have fallen off pace to more easily catch up.

6. **Is a book like *Talking Walls* needed?**

Maureen:	*Kilian:*
The book provides an immediate translation to recommendations or suggestions. For me, that is a great gift. My teaching life would have been easier if I had one of these my first year. While participating in this project to share our middle class school ideas, I have found strategies to use in this book.	Of course. While it is important to discuss the most effective classroom methodology, discussion is only a partial telling. By truly *showing* what the application of key principles look like in the classrooms of proven effective educators, we more fully promote the spread of ideas and their ultimate application.

Resources

"How To Protocol" for:

- Teaching Classroom Procedure
- Increasing Student Engagement
- Setting Up a Classroom Library
- Using Non-Linguistic Representations - Word Cards
- Setting Up Data Walls
- Developing Meta-Cognition with the New Blooms
- Teaching the Future
- 5 Levers for Creating a Safe and Productive Leaning Environment

Research and Reading Resources
Resources from the Authors

Resources: "How To" Protocol: Teaching Classroom Procedure

Classroom Rules and Procedures:

First, make a list of things that you have to do everyday together in the classroom. Make this manageable by:

1. Having students share their ideas in pairs or small groups first, listing their ideas on a white board, and then using the "no repeats" strategy for the share out. As each group shares, others check off the duplicate responses on their own lists and only share things that are different from the previous share.

2. Chunking the tasks by logical groups. List these on a large chart for reference.

   - Times of the day: when the bell rings, during lessons, getting ready for recess, lunch, getting ready to go home etc.

   - Types of tasks: homework, starting the day, during instruction, getting help, materials, books and library, etc.

Your categories may look something like this; however, the students may have another way in mind to organize this. The more they are involved in developing these descriptions of procedures, the more invested they will be in following the procedures.

Beginning the day • Homework turned in • Checking in books • Logging at-home reading • Getting materials ready for the day	**Getting along all day long** • Helping others • Keeping your hands to yourself • Walking in the classroom • Transitions—cleaning up, lining up • Getting bathroom breaks
Using materials in the classroom • Getting & sharpening pencils • Using the computer • Sharing text books • Using the art supply corner	**During instruction—getting help, participation** • Using attentive listening • Partner sharing • Using hand signals • What to do during an interruption • What to do when I am finished early
Working in small groups • Taking turns • Sharing materials • Listening to each other • Getting the job done (everyone)	**Getting ready to go home** • Homework materials • Cleaning up your desk • Lining up for the end of the day

Resources: "How To" Protocol: Teaching Classroom Procedure

Teaching a New Task

Use the following procedure to teach the task in a way that is understandable to everyone and includes participation in the development of the routine.

1. Use the Select the task.

2. Have the students role play on how to do it correctly and incorrectly. Students find it really amusing to view the negative example of an expected behavior. As the teacher, you may choose to be the one who does it "wrong" so the other students may have the fun of judging your performance and thereby reinforcing for themselves how to do things in the classroom.

3. List the steps for this dramatized procedure on a chart and keep it posted as long as needed to reinforce upon what was agreed.

4. If students stray from the expected procedure on the chart. You can simply point to the step they missed as a reminder.

This acting out and listing on a chart of classroom procedures is especially helpful to English learners who may not have understood verbal instructions and who may have come from schools with different codes of classroom behavior.

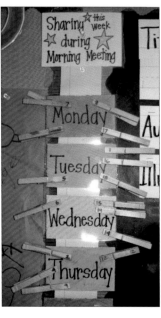
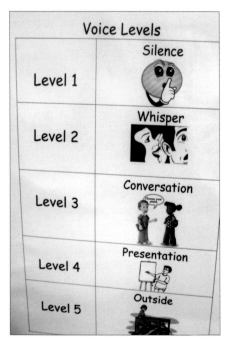

Resources: "How To" Protocol: Increasing Student Engagement

Increasing student engagement requires the use of interactive teaching strategies. These strategies will promote student engagement and active learning. They require students to demonstrate their understanding of instruction through active response.

As teachers, it is critical that we know if our instruction is successful. One way to do this is to periodically to 'take the pulse' of the classroom to see who is understanding the lesson and who needs more support. In other words, we need to check for understanding so we can adjust our instruction on the go. When interactive teaching strategies are used, you increase student interaction and student feedback per student per minute. You also increase teacher feedback per student per minute!

Student Engagement	Learning
Makes contact with the teacher	Experiences engagement and discovery
Participates in a variety of ways	Questions for understanding
1. Acknowledges teacher talking non-verbally	Connects prior experience and previous material covered in class
2. Follows non-verbal cues (thumbs up)	Participates due to content meaning, value, and future use in work or school
3. Offers opinions	Understands importance of tasks & processes in collaboration & independently
4. Restates information	Wants feedback and critique
5. Has materials on desk	Develops skill and knowledge over time
6. Follows directions	Improves with feedback
7. Utilizes time as prescribed	Seeks other resources to support learning
Presents interest in subject	Enjoys success

How Interactive Teaching Strategies are Applied in the Classroom

 **calling on** *ONE* **student for a response.** Promote active engagement in learning from all students.

Use One or More of the Following Alternative Strategies:

- White Boards
- Response cards – Yes, No, I agree, I disagree
- Signals
- Cooperative Talk Structures: Talk Tickets and more

Resources: "How To" Protocol: Increasing Student Engagement

White Boards

Use these to maximize engagement during lessons. Students can write words, phrases and sentences; draw a picture; or write a number or equation in response to your questions. White boards allow you to give feedback, check for understanding, redirect, and reinforce for the entire class better than any other tool.

Response Cards

Have students use response cards: **YES** or **NO**

These cards are best used when the answers are <u>NOT</u> clearly YES or NO. These cards are prompts for discussion.

Signals

Have students use signals to check for whole group response during a lesson. For example, "Use thumbs up if the word I say has the /i/ sounds, as in 'igloo'."

Resources: "How To" Protocol: Increasing Student Engagement

Talk Tickets

Any small object such as a paper clip, bingo marker, or paper 'ticket' can be used as a ticket to talk! The ticket buys you a chance to talk during a small group discussion. Each student receives the same number of Talk Tickets at the beginning of a small group discussion. As students enter into to the discussion, they place one token in the middle of the table. When they have expressed their thought or opinion, if they have another idea, they must place another token in the center of the table. When they have run out of tokens, their turn is over and it is the next person's turn. When everyone has run out of tokens, their talk time is up. They then can only make additional contributions **after** the others in the group have used up their tickets. Talk Tickets encourage participation in two ways: they restrict dominant students from monopolizing the discussion and they encourage reluctant students to share more of their ideas.

Resources: "How To" Protocol:
Setting Up a Classroom Library

Provide students with as **wide a range of reading materials** as possible.

A **good classroom library** should include:

- Up to 1500 titles (or 15-20 titles per student).

- Reading material for the range of levels of your students (usually 2 years below and two years above your grade level).

- A wide variety of genres—historical and realistic fiction, fairytales, science fiction, poetry, joke and riddle books, tall tales, etc.

- Series books—Harry Potter, Babysitters Club, Goosebumps, etc.

- Nonfiction material on a variety of topics of interest to the students, especially those linked to themes and targets that are standards.

- Magazines, newspapers and comic books, and prior student work

- Dictionaries and thesauruses usable by students

Have **reading material organized** in such a way that students can select and return books easily.

- Organize materials by reading level, genre, author, series, or topic.

- Sort books on shelves or in tubs.

- Create a labeling system so that students can select and return books easily. Color coding with dots is easy for all ages.

- Arrange the physical space of the library corner so that several students can browse books at the same time.

Resources: "How To" Protocol: Setting Up a Classroom Library

☐ Establish **ground rules** for independent reading time through role play, teacher modeling, and clearly posted rules and procedures. Many teachers have students select their books for independent reading BEFORE a recess so that when they come in to read, they can settle quickly. Walking around the classroom during independent reading time is discouraged so that all students can focus on quiet reading.

☐ Provide additional support to **foster independence** for students as needed. This may include help with selecting appropriate books, offering buddy reading of more difficult material, and reviewing strategies used to handle unknown words. *(See the Just Right Books posters in the Tool Kit, pages 112-118, and on the CD.)* Occasionally ask students to disclose what they are reading while in the full group.

☐ Allow **students to choose** what they would like to read during independent reading time. If the goal of any literacy program is to produce independent readers and writers who **choose to read** what interests them and fulfills their needs, then we must allow a time for this to occur on a daily basis. Providing choice gives students the opportunity to develop their own tastes and preferences as readers. Voluntary and free reading means that there is no "cost"—no book reports or other products should be required. However, praise and reinforcement should be plentiful!

☐ Hold **book talks** during independent reading time once per week. Students sign up to share their opinions with their peers about the books they are reading. This process generates increased student interest in reading a wide range of material.

Resources: "How To" Protocol:
Using Non-Linguistic Representations - Word Cards

Vocabulary word cards provide teachers with accurate visual prompts that are aligned with current scientific research for the value of non-linguistic representations (NLRs) in teaching, Marzano (2005). NLRs especially serve new readers, slow decoders, and English language learners. They are aids for vocabulary, prompts for predictions and definitions, supports for writing, and a means to front load content for both narrative and expository lessons.

Classroom teachers often find that their students do not have the necessary life experiences to conjure the images necessary to navigate, comprehend, and produce for their language arts program. Cuing the students with images can aid them to create background knowledge and trigger their prior experience, making the learning more meaningful and, therefore, retrievable.

This new understanding using the word cards provides the students with the necessary tools to approach the language arts curriculum, independent assignments, and the text in testing circumstances. We call it "visual literacy". Visual literacy is when students can *make sense of the content* of a lesson and *develop meaning* through non-linguistic lenses. Evidence of their learning occurs when students are asked to respond. They can communicate their understanding appropriately in speaking, writing, and testing venues.

In any curriculum, the teacher's job is to help to make the student capable of using a word in speech and writing. These are the *productive* functions in language while listening and reading are *receptive*. This means that listening and reading are taken in but are passive because they do not have to be shared. Speaking and writing are shared and are called *productive* because the nature of the act requires the student to produce. The word cards facilitate *productive* use of language and promote interaction.

Other non-linguistic tools recommended by the research are graphic organizers, doodles (from both students and teachers), realia such as bringing artifacts and "real world" applications into the classroom, and modeling of tasks and lessons. These tools help students to *see* what is needed and will be learned. The students report that they like taking "snapshots" of words and concepts. Seeing makes listening and "producing" easier.

(You will find references to "Testing Word Cards" and "College Word Cards" in the Tool Kit Section, pages 136 and 144 respectively. Both of these sets of word cards were developed by Michelle Karns and Charlotte Knox and are on the CD that comes with this booklet. Word Cards for use with Houghton-Mifflin and Open Court have been developed by Michelle Karns and are available through her at mskarns@pacbell.net.)

On the next five pages are some of the best ways we've found to use word cards.

Resources: "How To" Protocol: Using Non-Linguistic Representations - Word Cards

METHOD ONE: Say It - Show It - Spell It

One of the simplest ways to use these cards:

1. Show the WORD CARD with the printed word covered with a piece of sentence strip.

2. Ask the students what they think the word might be. Play with the students about the word. If it is a unique word, you might use a game of hangman to create a "muscle memory" for retrieval for the word. Let the students guess the word, predict what the word might be, or come up with synonyms for the word.

3. Tell the students the word and show the card in its entirety.

4. Say, "SAY it." Wait for a choral response of the word. Ask for it at least three times.

5. Dialogue about the word.

6. Provide the students with a simple kinesthetic definition of the word.

7. Say, "SHOW it."

8. Spell the word for the students. "SPELL it" Define it. Show it. Go through the cycle by calling it out.

9. "Boys and girls, Say it. Show it. Spell it."

10. Repeatedly call it out and ask for it in different sequences.

Resources: "How To" Protocol: Using Non-Linguistic Representations - Word Cards

METHOD TWO: Create, Compare, and Contrast

(You must be the judge of whether or not the word cards will lend themselves to this activity.)

1. Select a series of six to eight cards and based on the pictures alone and work with the students on telling stories.

2. Remind the students of the theme and how stories are constructed in the unit.

3. Let them take some time or work with a "buddy" to outline or develop a story line using the word cards as prompts.

4. After stories have been created and shared, provide an outline of the real upcoming anthology to be read in the theme.

5. Compare and contrast the stories made up from word cards and the actual story. Ask students, "Did the word cards reveal any aspect of the story?"

Another technique for the word cards is explicit vocabulary instruction preceding the experience of viewing the word in the story. This kind of front loading is recommended by Susanna Dutro and is a significant part of the English learners' arsenal for preparing for access to the core language arts program. There are five aspects of vocabulary knowledge that students need to have in order to meet the word in text and not be slowed while reading.

1. Immediate recognition of the word and an image with the meaning attached

2. Sense of the word in terms of part of speech and usage

3. Ideas about how to check for the context clues in the text to understand the use of the word in the current narrative

4. Student places value on the word and recognizes that it has an important role in the narrative or text

5. Word has been tagged as one that must be retrievable for assessment or future use

Resources: "How To" Protocol:
Using Non-Linguistic Representations - Word Cards

METHOD THREE: Direct Instruction

When using the explicit instruction of vocabulary, the Direct Instruction (DI) model is best. The components include: **Presentation**, **Highly Structured Practice**, **Guided Practice**, **Independent Practice** and **Assessment**. Overall, direct and explicit instruction should follow a schema of teacher led, teacher-student, student-student actions that lead to long term memory retention of the vocabulary words and an understanding of how to use the words in multiple settings.

☐ **I Do It:**

Teacher presents content and leads students in application activity.

☐ **We Do It:**

Students work with the teacher in less structured whole group practice.

☐ **You Do It:**

Students work with students to check personal understanding

☐ **We Check It:**

Formal and informal assessments are done for the students and for the teacher to ensure ongoing monitoring of progress, standards acquisition, and proficiency.

Students need to have a clear picture of the outcome of any assessment. It should provide them with specific information about what they need to work on and what they are doing well. Students should know what they already know and what they need to know.

Resources: "How To" Protocol:
Using Non-Linguistic Representations - Word Cards

METHOD FOUR: Icons

One of the student's favorite activities is the exchange of an actual WORD CARD for an icon.

1. Have the students look at the word card and then make up an icon for the word.

2. Then have students write a sentence using the icon instead of the word, just like hieroglyphics.

3. Have students trade off to see if they can "read" the icons their peers have made for the word cards in a vocabulary lesson. This really forces the students to use context clues and to understand the word. Besides, it is great fun!

4. You can make the lesson more difficult by taking the word cards down or turning them around so that they can't be used during the activity.

METHOD FIVE: Knowing the Word

1. Place all the WORD CARDS out for the story.

2. Explain what a "personal lexicon" is to the students. That is, vocabulary that is held in the "personal dictionary" in our brain. Here are five significant points to remember about learning words:

The math problem was

He could not figure it out.

- There are <u>many ways</u> to know a word.

- Sometimes <u>we recognize it but don't know what it means.</u>

- At times, we have <u>some understanding</u> of the word in one context but not others.

- Other times <u>we *know* the word</u> and understand it in <u>multiple contexts</u>.

- For a word to be committed to our personal lexicon, we want to <u>know as much as possible</u> about a word. When that happens, it is likely that we will be able to use it in our speech and writing.

3. Have the students look at each word and decide:
- ☐ **I never saw it before.**
- ☐ **I've heard it, but I don't know what it means.**
- ☐ **I recognize it in context,**
- ☐ **it has something to do with...**
- ☐ **I *know* it.**

> ### Levels of Word Knowledge
> #### (Stahl, 1999)
> - **I never saw it before.**
> - **I've heard it, but I don't know what it means.**
> - **I recognize it in context, it has something to do with...**
> - **I *know* it.**

Resources: "How To" Protocol:
Using Non-Linguistic Representations—Word Cards

1. Ask students to raise their hands for each decision to each word. Tally how many students raise their hands for each category.

2. Ask students who **know** the words to teach other students about the word and how it can be used in a variety of contexts.

3. Continue through all the words that were placed on the board until you all have a clear picture of the words that are known and unknown.

4. Dialogue with students where we get our familiarity with words.

5. Have students select words that they want to make sure they remember.

6. Ask students to write about how they will remember these words; what strategies they will use.

7. Have students share their solutions.

Word cards are very versatile. They can be used to enhance the understanding of the story from which they were chosen, or as simple flash cards for words students need to remember in any context. They can be used in the order of the curriculum, or randomly selected from throughout the disk. This versatility is a great benefit. The cards can be sorted and categorized and they can be used in small or large groups. They evoke background knowledge and support visual literacy.

Word cards allow students and teachers to join forces and meet the challenges of grade level standards through high expectations and rigorous assignments. This is one ancillary product the students themselves ask for and want to work with on a daily basis. They serve all four language domains because they can be used to help in listening, reading, writing and speaking. Using them, teachers and students together can create the magic that is learning.

Resources: "How To" Protocol: Setting Up Data Walls

A data wall is used when you want to present the progress on an IMPORTANT objective or academic goal. It is not to be used frivolously or for ALL objectives; it needs to be reserved for the academic concerns that are priorities for the entire class or grade level. When students are asked to monitor their own and their peer's progress they are being engaged in a sacred task of being a partner in one another's learning. This is a gift. Students who learn to consider and work well with others are better prepared for the curriculum transitions that occur after third grade when the objectives become more content-focused rather than skill-based.

When constructing a data wall, three discrete decisions need to be made before any action is taken. 1) What data will be used? 2) What is the purpose of the presentation? 3) How will the data be presented in the public forum and how will it be monitored? Let's look at one of the data presentations depicted in the photo montage.

1. **Data**: Words per minute to establish fluency.

2. **Purpose**: Motivate an increase in reading rate and comprehension.

3. **Presentation**: Use a metaphor of thermometer with rate shown increasing on scale and students will monitor their personal growth based on fluency tests.

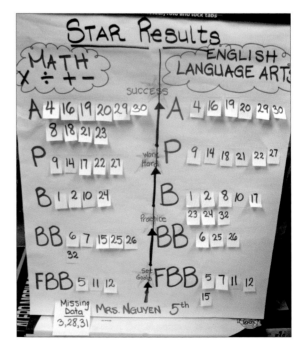

If the answers to the above questions are ambiguous, you will need to rethink whether or not you need to use a data wall. For example, teachers will sometimes make non-relevant data visual and take away from the importance of the data wall. Ask the students what data they want to monitor—they will tell you what they think is most important to the curriculum. If the data is sensitive, such as the performance levels in reading or math on the California Standards Test (CST), it is a good idea to give students or their representatives a voice in how the data will be presented in the public forum of the classroom and how the students will personally monitor their progress.

See the photo demonstrating how one class determined to present their CST information and the resulting performance levels from advanced, proficient, basic, below basic, and far below basic. Each student has a personal private number assigned to them that is used in the CST display. Progress can be monitored and the numbered slips moved up or down the performance levels based on the formative assessments in language arts and math conducted after the CST. Only the teacher and the student know who matches the number to name. In this case, the teacher must monitor the public posting and manage the movement of the student advancement or loss of performance status.

Resources: "How To" Protocol: Developing Meta-cognition with the New Bloom's Taxonomy

There are six categories in the new Bloom's Taxonomy. Each is headed with a verb rather than a noun. The verb heading gives a direction about what to do to meet the thinking objective for each domain. For example, you can teach the students how to use Bloom's Taxonomy by deconstructing a well-known story such as *The Three Little Pigs* or a story from the student's anthology. *(The Bloom's prompts are on pages 137-142 in this book and also on the CD.)*

Remember

- Ask the students what they remember about the story.
- Write down all comments on a poster-size chart paper.
- Challenge any comments that are inconsistent or not appropriate.
  - Ask, "Do you all agree?"
  - Allow students to check the facts if there is a need or disagreement.
- Continue until the story is retold with beginning—middle—end facts accurately recounted.
- Check with the students about accuracy and continuity.
- Make sure that there is agreement about the story.

Understand

- Debrief with the students.
- Ask what the main idea of the story was.
- Request evidence to support your idea.
- Identify different perspectives.
- Try to look at why there might be different ways of looking at the story.
- Generate consensus or agreements about central themes.

Apply

- Ask how the story applies to today's circumstances.
- Inquire about the different characters and who they might be as people in the news.
- Make the story parallel with current or historical events.
- Talk about the story as a metaphor for someone's life. Describe the life.

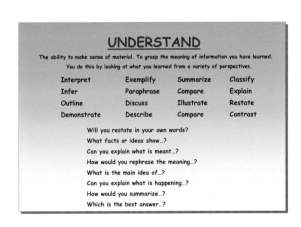

REMEMBER

The ability to restate, recall, and recognize previously learned material. You think about what was important and write it down.

Tell	Name	Locate	Describe	Identify
Explain	Retell	Define	List	Memorize
Label	Find	Match		

Who, what, why, where, when?
Name all the characters in the story.
How would you describe...?
Can you list three _____?
Write six facts from the story.
When/where does the story take place?
How does the story end?

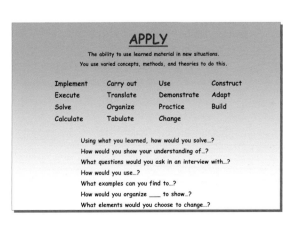

UNDERSTAND

The ability to make sense of material. To grasp the meaning of information you have learned. You do this by looking at what you learned from a variety of perspectives.

Interpret	Exemplify	Summarize	Classify
Infer	Paraphrase	Compare	Explain
Outline	Discuss	Illustrate	Restate
Demonstrate	Describe	Compare	Contrast

Will you restate in your own words?
What facts or ideas show...?
Can you explain what is meant...?
How would you rephrase the meaning...?
What is the main idea of...?
Can you explain what is happening...?
How would you summarize...?
Which is the best answer...?

APPLY

The ability to use learned material in new situations. You use varied concepts, methods, and theories to do this.

Implement	Carry out	Use	Construct
Execute	Translate	Demonstrate	Adapt
Solve	Organize	Practice	Build
Calculate	Tabulate	Change	

Using what you learned, how would you solve...?
How would you show your understanding of...?
What questions would you ask in an interview with...?
How would you use...?
What examples can you find to...?
How would you organize _____ to show...?
What elements would you choose to change...?

Resources: "How To" Protocol: Developing Meta-cognition with the New Bloom's Taxonomy

Analyze

- Request that the students compare and contrast the motivation of each character.

- Check your own feelings when you remembered the story.

- Ask a partner about their favorite character and determine why.

- Reflect on the author's purpose for writing the story, is it still valid?

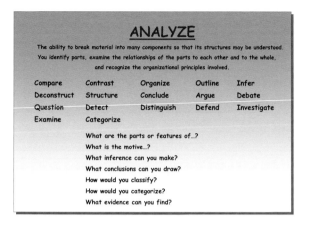

Evaluate

- Solicit opinions. Do you have a VOICE that needs to be heard regarding the story?

- Allow judgments. This is the opportunity phase of Bloom's Taxonomy; students have an opportunity to judge the story as long as they provide EVIDENCE to support their judgment.

- Support future forecasts. Ask students to talk about the author's future, the story's viability, and whether or not the people will know the story in fifty years?

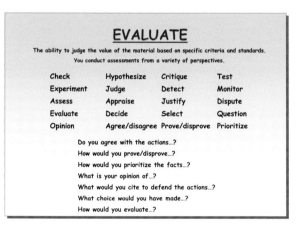

Create

- A new product needs to be brought forth from the experience of using the thoughtful process of Bloom's Taxonomy. The students can brainstorm what those products might look like – CHOICE at this point is really important and reflects the best of the research about thinking or cognitive processing.

- Students can work with partners or small groups. However, make sure that they identify how they are thinking to accomplish the tasks being completed.

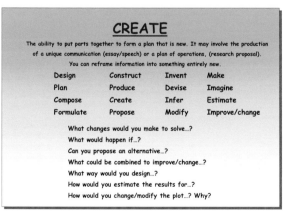

Resources: "How To" Protocol: 5 Levers for Creating a Safe and Productive Learning Environment

I. Rigorous Structure

Procedures

Maureen:

Detailed procedures, which I explicitly teach during the first three weeks of school, drive the fast-paced flow of my room. The most detailed procedures take place during the first 10 minutes of every period. Students enter the room and immediately take out their homework, pencil, and "**do now**". They write down the daily objective, homework, and **do now** questions. One student sets the timer for five minutes and when it sounds, gauges class completion of the **do now** by asking for a hand signal (i.e., "Raise one finger if you need one more minute"). After the time keeper informs me that the majority of students have completed their **do now**, I move the front of the room to share answers. Upon entering, the morning facilitator, another student, distributes post-its to pre-selected students. The four students write their answer to one of four **do now** questions on the post-it and place it on the board. When I reach the board, I share the answers on the post-its. Students "challenge" incorrect answers. After about three weeks, students take on the role of going through the **do now** answers. The first ten minutes is entirely student-driven.

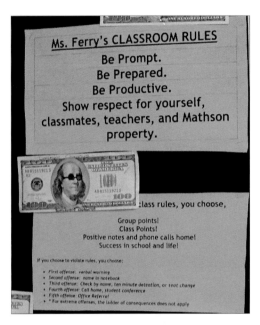

Kilian:

I use a series of hand-signals for common classroom things, based on ASL. "**B**" for bathroom requests, "**C**" for confusion, "**G**" for throwing things in the garbage requests, "**Q**" to take computer quizzes, "**W**" to drink water, etc. This greatly speeds the request-response equation, and eliminates potential distraction, allowing the class to stay focused and on task.

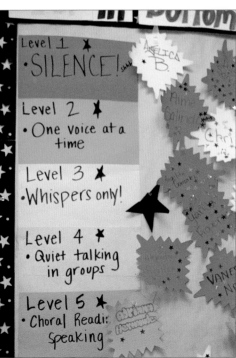

Resources: "How To" Protocol: 5 Levers for Creating a Safe and Productive Learning Environment

I. Rigorous Structure

Predictable Daily and Weekly Cycles

Maureen:

At the beginning of each week, students receive a weekly packet. The front page of the packet includes a grid where students create a weekly goal and self-assess daily on the categories of participation, in-class work, preparedness, and respect. The last two minutes of every class period are used for students to self-assess and calculate their "daily GPA." The packet also includes a template for students' **do now**s for the week, as well as their closers for the end each day. The last page of the packet lists vocabulary words for the week.

Kilian:

Each day follows the same pattern: skill review from previous weeks, spelling and vocabulary practice, phonics and fluency practice, front-loading of new concepts, grammar/ writing, reading strategies/ literature analysis, and independent reading. Rarely, do we deviate.

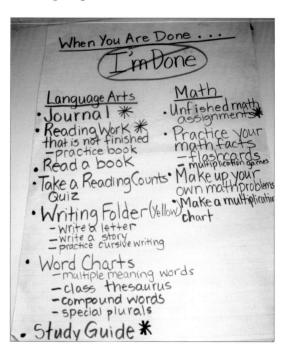

Consistent Teach-Practice-Assess Cycles

Kilian:

Every week students are expected to learn a set of spelling words, a set of vocabulary words, 1-2 affixes, a grammar/ writing concept, and a reading strategy or literature analysis skill. Concepts are introduced on Mondays, deepened on Tuesdays and Wednesdays, practiced extensively on Thursday, and assessed in a variety of ways on Fridays.

Resources: "How To" Protocol: 5 Levers for Creating a Safe and Productive Learning Environment

I. Rigorous Structure

Categorized Activities

Maureen:

Note-taking, which occurs Monday through Thursday, follows the same daily structure. I use symbols to represent the various stages in the lesson and note-taking process. The lesson starts with the daily objective (e.g., "By the end of today, I will be able to add fractions with unlike denominators"), which is represented with a target symbol. Key points follow and are represented with a star. Examples, represented by an "**x**" in a box follow, as do guided practice problems we work through together, represented by a hand. A pencil symbol signifies independent practice problems. Lastly, a door represents the closer, a mini-assessment to measure students' mastery of the daily objective. Whether notes are presented using

PowerPoint®, posters, or the white board, structures and symbols remain the same.

Kilian:

The purpose of the activity (new instruction, practice, review, assessment) drives its structure. We review old skills in a variety of ways, but the *way in which* we **review** is always distinct from the *way in which* we **learn new material**, which in turn is distinct from the *way in which* we **practice material**.

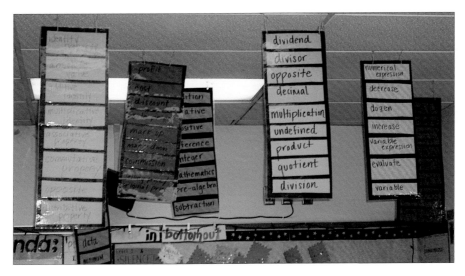

Resources: "How To" Protocol: 5 Levers for Creating a Safe and Productive Learning Environment

II. Opportunities to Experience Success

Skill-Based Diagnostics

Maureen:

I administer a basic skills math assessment 3 times per year. The results help me target the greatest deficits in skills and teach in a way that bridges the gap between my students' skill level and grade-level content.

Instruction Targeted To Student Needs

Maureen:

Each day after the **do now**, we do a "mad minute," a one-minute basic skills practice set. The skill changes depending on the current content.

Kilian:

We obviously teach in a standards-based context, but in order to ready students for instruction that is *on*-standard, we often need to teach skills that are *pre*-standard. Sometimes, we have to teach *pre*-standard skills for substantial periods of time. This does not demonstrate lowering expectations, or dumbing down curriculum. It is an example of providing students with the exact instruction they need to achieve academically, and is a powerful tool for raising student achievement.

Smart is not something you _are_, smart is something you _get_.

Resources: "How To" Protocol:
5 Levers for Creating a Safe and
Productive Learning Environment

II. Opportunities to Experience Success

Front-Loading/Scaffolding/Pre-Teaching

Kilian:

Scaffolding is a critical component of my instruction. I continuously break down performance tasks into ever smaller and more discrete skills. These skills are taught, practiced, and assessed independently, allowing students to demonstrate continued learning that leads toward mastery of the ultimate performance target.

Resources: "How To" Protocol:
5 Levers for Creating a Safe and Productive Learning Environment

III. Celebration and Recognition of Growth

Establish Big Goals

Maureen:

(1) Improve basic math skill level by at least two years.

(2) Maintain an 80% mastery average on all grade-level skills.

(3) Score proficient or advanced on the California Standardized Test.

(4) Get on the College Track.

Kilian:

(1) Improve writing 1 point on the 4-point rubric.

(2) Master 80% of all content skills.

(3) Improve independent reading level two grade levels.

(4) Read 180 words per minute.

(These goal formats are in the Tool Kit Section, pages 146-149 and on the CD.)

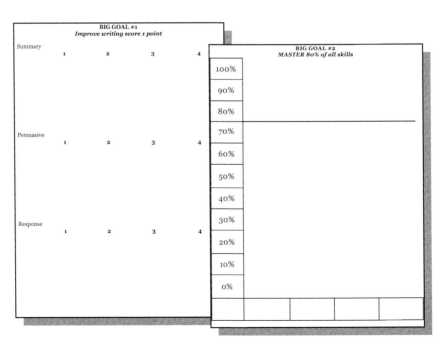

Resources: "How To" Protocol: 5 Levers for Creating a Safe and Productive Learning Environment

III. Celebration and Recognition of Growth

Track Progress Incrementally and Transparently

Maureen:

I provide students with data on skill mastery every Monday. I invite students who earn a 100% on a skill quiz, to "become a member" of the **100 Club**. They earn a star with their name on it to add to the **100 Club board**. With each additional 100%, I invite them to "update their membership" by adding a sticker to their star. After five 100 percents, students earn a fake $100 bill to add to the board. More importantly, students earn "baller status," a highly sought after recognition. Beginning every Monday with this celebratory structure starts each week off positively. All students have the opportunity to re-take skills quizzes if they did not earn 100%.

Kilian:

I provide students with data on skill mastery each week. They update reading strategy mastery twice quarterly. They update progress toward **Big Goals** six times a year. Students keep charts with data that reveal progress toward all these key performance areas, and so they know where they stand academically at all times.

Resources: "How To" Protocol: 5 Levers for Creating a Safe and Productive Learning Environment

III. Celebration and Recognition of Growth

Student Ownership of Progress Monitoring

Kilian:

Students must use the progress monitoring data and charts they keep. In my classroom, students use their English Experts tracking sheets to determine which skills they need to retake on weekly assessments, and whether or not they need to attend key review sessions. They use reading strategies tracking sheets to determine which strategies to practice on weekly reading logs.

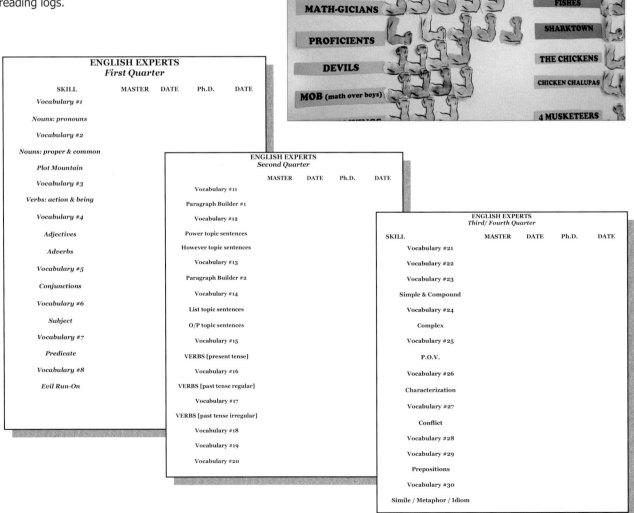

ENGLISH EXPERTS
First Quarter

SKILL	MASTER	DATE	Ph.D.	DATE
Vocabulary #1				
Nouns: pronouns				
Vocabulary #2				
Nouns: proper & common				
Plot Mountain				
Vocabulary #3				
Verbs: action & being				
Vocabulary #4				
Adjectives				
Adverbs				
Vocabulary #5				
Conjunctions				
Vocabulary #6				
Subject				
Vocabulary #7				
Predicate				
Vocabulary #8				
Evil Run-On				

ENGLISH EXPERTS
Second Quarter

SKILL	MASTER	DATE	Ph.D.	DATE
Vocabulary #11				
Paragraph Builder #1				
Vocabulary #12				
Power topic sentences				
However topic sentences				
Vocabulary #13				
Paragraph Builder #2				
Vocabulary #14				
List topic sentences				
O/P topic sentences				
Vocabulary #15				
VERBS [present tense]				
Vocabulary #16				
VERBS [past tense regular]				
Vocabulary #17				
VERBS [past tense irregular]				
Vocabulary #18				
Vocabulary #19				
Vocabulary #20				

ENGLISH EXPERTS
Third/ Fourth Quarter

SKILL	MASTER	DATE	Ph.D.	DATE
Vocabulary #21				
Vocabulary #22				
Vocabulary #23				
Simple & Compound				
Vocabulary #24				
Complex				
Vocabulary #25				
P.O.V.				
Vocabulary #26				
Characterization				
Vocabulary #27				
Conflict				
Vocabulary #28				
Vocabulary #29				
Prepositions				
Vocabulary #30				
Simile / Metaphor / Idiom				

Resources: "How To" Protocol: 5 Levers for Creating a Safe and Productive Learning Environment

IV. Reflections of Students in Class Practices

Humor

Kilian:

The middle school kid is, among other things, goofy. Those that are not goofy tend to appreciate all things silly, ridiculous, or gross. Accordingly, sample homework questions lean toward the absurd, my bathroom pass is a wooden shrimp named Ceviche, and my pre-directions routine involves standing on a chair wearing a pirate hat while the class shouts, "Aye! Aye! Cap'n!"

Resources: "How To" Protocol: 5 Levers for Creating a Safe and Productive Learning Environment

IV. Reflections of Students in Class Practices

What's Now

Maureen:

I'm thinking about a specific example. In a unit on percents, my students design storefront windows of their favorite, or made-up, stores. The storefronts include a variety of merchandise, all priced differently. To practice calculating mark-ups and discounts, I hang the store windows around the room, turn on music, and students walk around "window-shopping" while calculating discounts and mark-ups. I also share a similar taste in music with my students and try to play music during all independent activities.

Kilian:

As a teacher, it isn't hard to include examples of whatever is popular in music, movies, T.V., food, clothing, etc., in class work, examples, homework, and assessments. This doesn't mean a teacher needs to enjoy or appreciate these things, nor does it necessarily entail turning one's classroom into a giant pop culture museum, but the carefully placed allusion and example can go a long way.

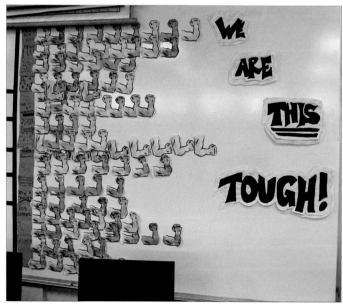

Resources: "How To" Protocol: 5 Levers for Creating a Safe and Productive Learning Environment

V. High Behavioral and Academic Expectations

Choice

Maureen:

In addition to presenting basic classroom rules at the beginning of the year, I infuse the element of choice into student behavior and academic performance. They can *choose* to follow the rules, complete all in-class assignments and homework to reap the rewards. The rewards include positive notes and phone calls home, group and class points, a stronger brain, and a higher grade. Students can also *choose* to break rules and endure the class consequences. If students *choose* to bring incomplete homework to class, they know we will call home immediately and share with their parents/guardians their choice. The element of choice gives students the responsibility of shaping their experience in my class and empowers them to do well.

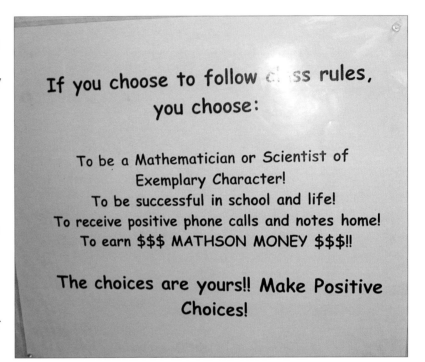

If you choose to follow class rules, you choose:

To be a Mathematician or Scientist of Exemplary Character!
To be successful in school and life!
To receive positive phone calls and notes home!
To earn $$$ MATHSON MONEY $$$!!

The choices are yours!! Make Positive Choices!

Resources: "How To" Protocol: 5 Levers for Creating a Safe and Productive Learning Environment

V. High Behavioral and Academic Expectations

Themes

Maureen:

My theme for my 8th graders is "Are you on the College Track?" I introduce it on Day 1 and we refer to it nearly every day after. We discuss how their 8th grade scores impact their high school placement courses, which can determine whether or not they are on the college track. The header of every assignment, quiz, and assessment in my class reads, "Are you on the College Track?"

Kilian:

Mine is **3-in-1**, which stands for three years of academic growth in a singular school year. This theme becomes our over-arching purpose, and is used as **motivation** (*We need to go 3-in-1 to be ready for high school*); **encouragement** (*If we keep working like this we'll all go 3-in-1*) and a tool to

refocus behavior (*This is not the way students who go 3-in-1 act*). Moreover, it is a single powerful message to send to both students and families that clearly articulates what we are about and why we do what we do.

(Copies of the icons and forms from these middle school experts are available in the Tool Kit, pages 145-155, and on the CD.)

Who are you?
Who will you become?

Leave your mark.

Intelligence is not fixed; hard work and building your vocabulary increases intelligence.

Resources: "How To" Protocol: 5 Levers for Creating a Safe and Productive Learning Environment

V. High Behavioral and Academic Expectations

Relationships

Kilian:

Relationships are the prerequisites for relentlessly holding kids to the highest of expectations. In the absence of positive rapport, this type of no excuses attitude engenders significant student pushback, but once relationships are established, teachers need to do *less* to maintain high expectations. The kids take themselves there.

Maureen:

I could not have stated it better. Ditto.

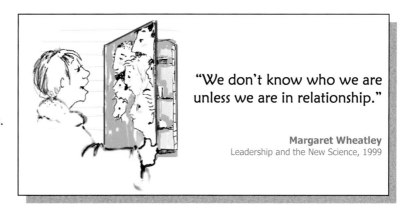

"We don't know who we are unless we are in relationship."

Margaret Wheatley
Leadership and the New Science, 1999

The Path of Relationship

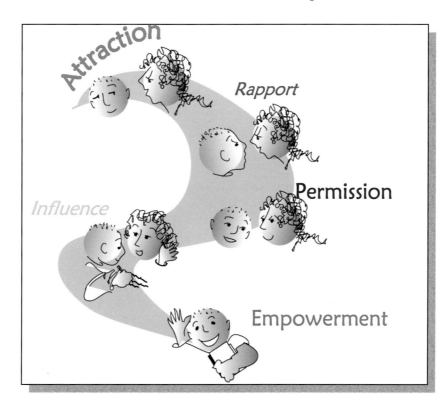

Research and Reading Resources

Along with our own experience in school reform and working in the classroom, there are several researchers to whom we have turned for data, resources, and experience to help us do what we do. We have referred to the work of several of them in this book. Here is a list of the resources we feel will benefit you in using the principles outlined in this book.

Bloom's Taxonomy:

Anderson, L.W. & Krathwohl (Eds.) (2001).A Taxonomy for Learning, Teaching, and Assessing: A Revision of Bloom's Taxonomy of Educational Objectives. New York: Longman.

Resiliency:

Benard, Bonnie. (2004). Resiliency: What We Have Learned. WestEd.

Benard, Bonnie; Henderson, Nan; Sharp-Light, Nancy. (1999). Resiliency in Action: Practical Ideas for Overcoming Risks and Building Strengths in Youth, Families & Communities. Resiliency in Action, Inc.

Benard, Bonnie. (1996) "Fostering Resiliency in Kids: Protective Factors in the Family, School, and Community." Portland, OR: Western Regional Center for Drug-Free Schools and Communities, 1991, as quoted in Resiliency in Action: A Journal of Application and Research, Winter, 1996, Rio Rancho, NM.

Werner, Emmy. (Winter 1996). "How Children Become Resilient," in Resiliency in Action: A Journal of Application and Research. Rio Rancho, NM.

Standards:

T.H.E. Journal on the Internet: http://thejournal.com/the/magazine

Reform:

Garmezy, N. (1991). "Resiliency and vulnerability to adverse developmental outcomes associated with poverty." American Behavioral Scientist, 34(4), 416-430.

Noddings, N. (2003). Caring: A feminine approach to ethics and moral education. Berkeley: University of California Press.

Rutter, M. (1987). "Psychosocial resilience and protective mechanisms." American Journal of Orthopsychiatry: 57, 316-331.

Seligman, M.; with Reivich, K; Jaycox, L. & Gillham, J. (1995). Optimistic Child: A Revolutionary Program That Safeguards Children Against Depression and Builds Lifelong Resiliency. New York: Houghton-Mifflin.

Research and Reading Resources

Vocabulary:

Beck, I. L.; McKeown, M. G. & Kucan, L. (2002). Bringing words to life: Robust vocabulary instruction. New York: Guilford.

Becker, W. C. (1977). Teaching reading and language to the disadvantaged – What we have learned from field research. Harvard Educational Review, 47, 518-543.

Elley, W. (1989). Vocabulary acquisition from listening to stories. Reading Research Quarterly, 24, 174-187.

Krashen, S. (1993). The case for free, voluntary reading. Canadian Modern Language Review, 50(1), 72-82.

Moats, L. C. (2001). Overcoming the language gap. American Educator, 25, 5, 8-9.

Nagy, W. E.; Anderson, R. C.; Schommer, M.; Scott, J. A. & Stallman, A. (1989). Morphological families in the internal lexicon. Reading Research Quarterly, 24, 262-282.

Shefelbine, J. (1990). Student factors related to variability in learning word meanings from context. Journal of Reading Behavior, 221, 71-97.

Snow, C.; Barnes, W. S.; Chandler, J.; Goodman, I. F. & Hemphill, L. (2000). Unfilled expectations: Home and school influences on literacy. Cambridge, MA: Harvard University Press.

Snow, C. E.; Tabors, P. O.; Nicholson, P. A. & Kurland, B. F. (1995). SHELL: Oral language and early literacy skills in kindergarten and first grade children. Journal of Research in Childhood Education, 10, 37-48.

Stahl, S. A. (in press). Four problems with teaching word meanings (and what to do to make vocabulary an integral part of instruction). In E. H. Hiebert & M. Kamil (Eds.), Teaching and learning vocabulary: Bringing scientific research to practice. Mahwah, NJ: Erlbaum.

Stahl, S. A. (1999). Vocabulary development. Cambridge, MA: Brookline Books.

Stahl, S. A., & Nagy, W. E. (2000). Promoting vocabulary development. Austin: Texas Education Agency.

Weizman, Z. O. & Snow, C. E. (2001). "Lexical input as related to children's vocabulary acquisition: Effects of sophisticated exposure and support for meaning." Developmental Psychology, 37, 265-279.

Resources from the Authors

Charlotte Knox, Knox Education:

Charlotte has made a number of helpful documents available for free download on her Web Ssite:

- Cooperative Talk Cards — visuals and directions for implementing 12 different talk structures in groups
- Academic Vocabulary Lists — all 7000+ terms in separate files by subject and grade level essential to academic success K-12
- Supports for success with the California Standards Test: academic terms and phrases based on the CST by grade level and subject, released test question grids correlate the standards to the format of the test item on the CST, test strategy posters are colorful, fun reminders of effective test-taking strategies
- California Standards-based writing rubrics for all genres
- The Night Writing Project: This is a fun practice process that brings students into writing with ease, creativity, and a great deal of enthusiasm. It is not a substitute for writing instruction, nor is it simply more "homework;" it is a way to "hook" students into writing meaningfully. Students receive a new writing prompt and supporting graphic organizers, revision ideas, and editing checklists for each weekly packet on Monday. Teachers provide a mini-lesson each day that guides that night's step in the writing process.

Access to the above items is free once you register at the site: www.knoxeducation.com. Current clients of Knox Education will be automatically given access via login through their member control panel. Others may purchase the book, "Backwards Planning for Success with Writing," or attend workshops which provide training in the process and in-class demonstrations of the mini-lessons.

Michelle Karns, Michelle Karns Consulting:

Michelle has developed hundreds of learning and teaching tools for students and teachers. Among them, she has developed word cards for use with the vocabulary words in the Houghton Mifflin and Open Court Reading Programs K-5 and K-6. The words are sorted by story and theme within the program. Each card includes the word typed in bold print and an illustration that is a photo or graphic to make the term understandable and memorable for the students.

She also developed word cards for use with testing and for fostering discussions on the future, on career, college, or training. Both of these sets of word cards are available on the CD provided with this book. A discussion of how to use word cards effectively is on pages 80-85.

Michelle has written several other books highlighting her work in education and the effective strategies that work.

1992 *The Trick Bag: A Handbook for Anyone Reaching Out to Kids*, which was later re-released as-

1993 *How to Create Positive Relationships with Students: A Handbook of Group Activities and Teaching Strategies*   (available through Research Press)

1995 *Why the Drug War Fails*, United Nations Presentation in the World Conference on Children

1995 *Doisms: Ten Prosocial Principles that Ensure Caring Connections with Kids*

1997 Paper: *"The Tulsa Title I Resiliency Project: Hope for the Future,"* Education Exchange, Vol.3 No.5

1997 *ProTactics: The Integration of Resiliency into the Classroom*

1998 *Ethnic Barriers and Biases: How to Become an Agent for Change*

The books *Doisms* and *Ethnic Barriers and Biases* are available in limited quantities directly from Michelle.

Michelle Karns Consulting	Phone 530-758-1997
P. O. Box 2155	Email: mskarns@pacbell.net
Davis, CA 95617-2155	Web Site: www.karnsconsulting.com

Talking Walls
Tool Kit

In a Perfect Classroom...

What do you see?

What do you hear?

What do you feel?

Conversation Norms

 Make sure your voice can be heard

 Talk to each other, not just to the teacher

 Listen to each other

 Take turns in the conversation

Don't interrupt or "talk over" the speaker

Advanced Conversation Norms

 Link your comments to the speaker before you end

 Wait until a topic is finished before changing topics

 If you state an opinion, you have to back it up or say you're not sure about it

 Avoid *monopolizing* (taking over) the conversation

 You can disagree, but show respect for others' ideas

STUDENT CREED

I am polite and courteous.
I am respectful.
I am responsible.
I am safe.
I am prepared.

We are here to learn; therefore,
I will do nothing to keep the teacher
from teaching and anyone from learning.

I will cooperate
with all school people,
respect myself, others and the environment.
By acting this way,
I am taking charge of my future.

If it is to be,
it is up to me.

I CAN DO IT!

Reading Success!

Comprehension

Developing Vocabulary	Increasing Word Recognition	Using Prior Knowledge	Learning Academic Language	Recognizing Text Structure/ Story Structure	Using Visualiza- tion/ Mental Imagery	Clarifying	Monitoring for Understand- ing	Summing Up
Identifying Main Idea	Making Connections	Using Graphic & Semantic Organizers	Predicting	Re-Reading Re-Telling	Discerning Important Information	Generating & Answering Questions	Interpreting	

Fluency

Increasing accuracy	Increasing rate	Using expression & intonation	Automatically recognizing words	Focusing on meaning	Utilizing choral reading, partner reading, tape-assisted reading
Using "chunking"	Pausing appropriately	Monitoring oral reading	Repeating reading (4X)	Making word connections	

Vocabulary

Building vocabulary indirectly & directly	Utilizing all types: listening, speaking, reading, writing	Tiering: casual, formal, domain specific	Learning word families	Identifying word parts: affixes, prefixes, suffixes	Identifying word parts: word roots, base words
Utilizing context clues	Using words in varied contexts	Acknowledging multiple-meaning Words	Making connections	Using dictionaries & other reference aids	Differentiating descriptive & expressive language

Phonics

Using alphabetic knowledge	Identifying short vowels in CVC words	Identifying short vowels, digraphs, -tch trigraph	Using vowel diphthongs	Using consonant sounds	Using R & L controlled vowels	Learning multi-syllabic words
Identifying letter names UPPERCASE & lowercase	Learning relationships between letters & sounds	Using long vowel sounds; short vowel sounds	Blending sounds to form words	Breaking spoken words into sounds	Learning vowel/letter sound relationships	Learning consonant/ letter sound relationships

Phonemic Awareness

Identifying & making rhymes	Using rime	Identifying beginning sounds same/different	Manipulating individual sounds	Using beginning/ending sound isolation	Using sound blending
Using sound/phoneme	Isolating phonemes	Identifying phonemes	Categorizing	Substituting	Manipulating phonemes

Concepts About Print

Identifying title, author, table of contents	Reading left to right, top to bottom	Learning that printed materials provide information or tell a story	Learning uppercase & lowercase letters	Using capital letters at beginning of a sentence and periods at the end

LANGUAGE
"Sea of Talk"
Marie Clay

Choosing Just Right Books
Five Finger Test

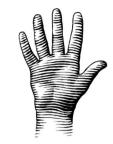

Sometimes it is difficult to know if a book is going to be too easy or too hard by just looking at it. The Five Finger test is one way to "test" a book before you spend too much time with it and get frustrated.

1) First, choose the book you think you would like to read.

2) Find a page of text somewhere in the middle of the book. Find a page with lots of text (words) and few or no pictures.

3) Begin to read the page. It is best to read the page aloud or in a whisper, if possible, while doing the test so you can hear the places where you have difficulty.

4) Each time you come to a word you don't know, hold one finger up.

5) If you have all five fingers up before you get to the end of the page, wave the book "good-bye." It is probably too difficult for you right now. Try it again later in the year. If you need help finding a book, ask your teacher or librarian.

6) If you have no fingers up when you finish the page, then the book may be an easy read for you. Use the Goldilocks' method as you read to see if the book is too easy or "just right." Enjoy!

7) If you have fewer than five fingers but more than one or two fingers up when you finish reading the page, the book may be just what you need to grow as a reader. Use the Goldilocks' method as you read to see if the book is a "just right" book. Enjoy!

Finding a "Just Right" Book

Do you remember Goldilocks' quest in the fairytale "Goldilocks and the Three Bears" to find the porridge, chair, and bed that were "just right"?

Selecting a book can sometimes feel the same way. Just as Goldilocks found that some porridges were too hot or too cold and others were just right, beginning readers often have difficulty finding books that are "just right" and not too hard or too easy.

When you are reading a book you can try asking yourself these questions to help you find a book that is "just right" for you.

Too Easy Books

As you read, ask yourself these questions. If you answer "yes" to most of the questions, then the book is probably too easy for you. You can still have fun reading it, but next time, try to choose a book that is a little more challenging.

1. Have you read this book many times before?
2. Do you understand the story very well without much effort?
3. Do you know and understand almost every word?
4. Can you read it smoothly and fluently without much practice or effort?

Just Right Books

As you read, ask yourself these questions. If you answer "yes" to most of them, then the book you are reading is probably "just right" for you. These are the books that will help you make the most progress in your reading. Read, enjoy and learn from the experience!

1. Is this book new to you?

2. Do you understand most of the book?

3. Are there a few words per page that you don't recognize or know the meaning to instantly? Remember to use the five finger test.

4. Can someone help you with the book if you hit a tough spot?

Too Hard Books

As you read ask yourself these questions, if you find that you answer "yes" to most of these questions, then the book is probably too hard for you. Don't forget about the book; just try it again later. As you gain experience in choosing "just right" books, you may find when you pick the book up again that it is "just right"

1. Are there more than a few words on a page that you don't recognize or know the meaning? Remember the five finger test.

2. Are you confused about what is happening in most of the book?

3. When you read are you struggling and does it sound choppy?

4. Is everyone busy and unable to help you if you hit a tough spot?

Too Easy Books

- Have you read this book many times before?

- Do you understand the story very well without much effort?

- Do you know and understand almost every word?

- Can you read it smoothly and fluently without much practice or effort?

Just Right Books

- Is this book new to you?

- Do you understand most of the book?

- Are there a few words per page that you don't know? Remember to use the five finger test.

- Can someone help you with the book if you hit a tough spot?

Too Hard Books

- Are there more than a few words on a page that you don't know? Remember the five finger test.

- Are you confused about what is happening in most of the book?

- When you read are you struggling and does it sound choppy?

- Is everyone busy and unable to help you if you hit a tough spot?

Dream books:

- I am confused about what is happening in the book.

- There are many words I don't know.

- My reading is choppy.

- I would like someone to read the book to me.

5 Star Writing
Checklists

These checklists are used to evaluate students' writing that will be placed on our writing portfolio wall. Each month the students place one of their published pieces on the writing wall. The piece must have 4 or 5 stars to go up on the wall. Fewer stars and they need to go back and rewrite it to fix mistakes.

Each month I make a new rubric based on what we are focusing on, the genre of the writing, and grade level expectations. I also change the symbol each month (5 stars, 5 smiles, 5 hearts…).

I put a star for each item they meet. The little slip gets glued at the bottom of their writing and put on the wall. There is also a chart-size copy of the checklist on the wall for students to refer to when they are writing.

General 5 Star Checklist
(good for beginning of the year)

 Punctuation

. ? ! "
,

 Capitals only where they go
- Beginning of sentence
- Names
- Months
- Days of the week

 Spelling
- All word wall words
- Harder words spelled using the sound cards

 Spaces between all words

 Paper is Neat
- Handwriting
- No smudges

 Punctuation

. ? ! "
,

 Capitals only where they go
- Beginning of sentence
- Names
- Months
- Days of the week

 Spelling
- All word wall words
- Harder words spelled using the sound cards

 Spaces between all words

 Paper is Neat
- Handwriting
- No smudges

Punctuation

. ? ! "
,

Capitals only where they go
- Beginning of sentence
- Names
- Months
- Days of the week

Spelling
- All word wall words
- Harder words spelled using the sound cards

Spaces between all words

Paper is Neat
- Handwriting
- No smudges

 Punctuation

. ? ! "
,

 Capitals only where they go
- Beginning of sentence
- Names
- Months
- Days of the week

 Spelling
- All word wall words
- Harder words spelled using the sound cards

 Spaces between all words

 Paper is Neat
- Handwriting
- No smudges

Paragraph 5 Star Checklist

Paragraphs	**Punctuation**	**Capitals only where they go**	**Spelling**	**Neat and clean handwriting**
• Indented • Topic Sentence • 3 supporting details • Closing Sentence	• Periods • Question marks • Exclamation points • Commas • Apostrophes	• Beginning of sentence • Names • Months • Days of the week	• All word wall words • All 3, 4, and 5 letter words	
Paragraphs	**Punctuation**	**Capitals only where they go**	**Spelling**	**Neat and clean handwriting**
• Indented • Topic Sentence • 3 supporting details • Closing Sentence	• Periods • Question marks • Exclamation points • Commas • Apostrophes	• Beginning of sentence • Names • Months • Days of the week	• All word wall words • All 3, 4, and 5 letter words	
Paragraphs	**Punctuation**	**Capitals only where they go**	**Spelling**	**Neat and clean handwriting**
• Indented • Topic Sentence • 3 supporting details • Closing Sentence	• Periods • Question marks • Exclamation points • Commas • Apostrophes	• Beginning of sentence • Names • Months • Days of the week	• All word wall words • All 3, 4, and 5 letter words	
Paragraphs	**Punctuation**	**Capitals only where they go**	**Spelling**	**Neat and clean handwriting**
• Indented • Topic Sentence • 3 supporting details • Closing Sentence	• Periods • Question marks • Exclamation points • Commas • Apostrophes	• Beginning of sentence • Names • Months • Days of the week	• All word wall words • All 3, 4, and 5 letter words	

Letter Writing 5 Star Checklist

Parts of a Letter

All parts are in their correct spot
- date
- greeting/salutation
- body
- closing
- signature

Punctuation
- Comma in the date, in the greeting, and in the closing
- All other punctuation is correct

? ! " , '

Capitals only where they go
- Beginning of sentence
- Names
- Months
- Days of the week
- Proper nouns

Spelling
- All word wall words
- Harder words spelled using the sound cards

Paper is Neat
- Spaces between all words
- Neat Handwriting (tall letters tall and short letters short)
- No smudges

Parts of a Letter

All parts are in their correct spot
- date
- greeting/salutation
- body
- closing
- signature

Punctuation
- Comma in the date, in the greeting, and in the closing
- All other punctuation is correct

? ! " , '

Capitals only where they go
- Beginning of sentence
- Names
- Months
- Days of the week
- Proper nouns

Spelling
- All word wall words
- Harder words spelled using the sound cards

Paper is Neat
- Spaces between all words
- Neat Handwriting (tall letters tall and short letters short)
- No smudges

Parts of a Letter

All parts are in their correct spot
- date
- greeting/salutation
- body
- closing
- signature

Punctuation
- Comma in the date, in the greeting, and in the closing
- All other punctuation is correct

? ! " , '

Capitals only where they go
- Beginning of sentence
- Names
- Months
- Days of the week
- Proper nouns

Spelling
- All word wall words
- Harder words spelled using the sound cards

Paper is Neat
- Spaces between all words
- Neat Handwriting (tall letters tall and short letters short)
- No smudges

Parts of a Letter

All parts are in their correct spot
- date
- greeting/salutation
- body
- closing
- signature

Punctuation
- Comma in the date, in the greeting, and in the closing
- All other punctuation is correct

? ! " , '

Capitals only where they go
- Beginning of sentence
- Names
- Months
- Days of the week
- Proper nouns

Spelling
- All word wall words
- Harder words spelled using the sound cards

Paper is Neat
- Spaces between all words
- Neat Handwriting (tall letters tall and short letters short)
- No smudges

"How to" Writing Checklist

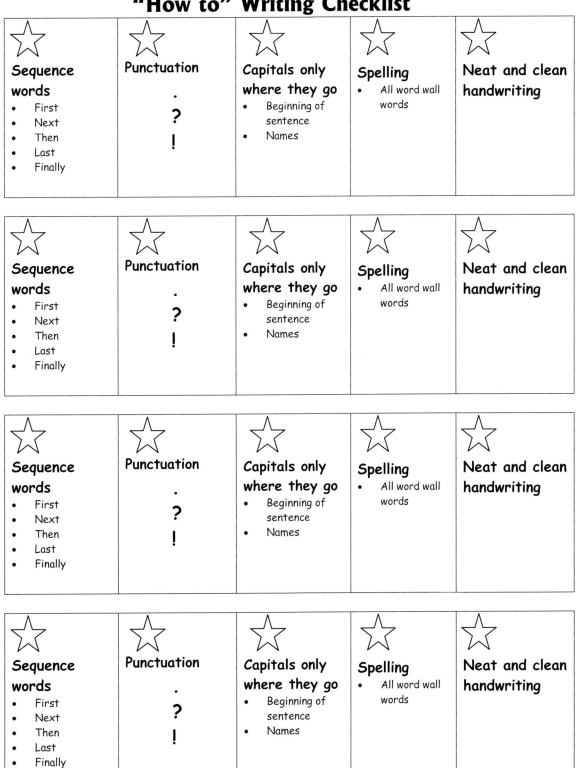

☆ Sequence words
- First
- Next
- Then
- Last
- Finally

☆ Punctuation
.
?
!

☆ Capitals only where they go
- Beginning of sentence
- Names

☆ Spelling
- All word wall words

☆ Neat and clean handwriting

☆ Sequence words
- First
- Next
- Then
- Last
- Finally

☆ Punctuation
.
?
!

☆ Capitals only where they go
- Beginning of sentence
- Names

☆ Spelling
- All word wall words

☆ Neat and clean handwriting

☆ Sequence words
- First
- Next
- Then
- Last
- Finally

☆ Punctuation
.
?
!

☆ Capitals only where they go
- Beginning of sentence
- Names

☆ Spelling
- All word wall words

☆ Neat and clean handwriting

☆ Sequence words
- First
- Next
- Then
- Last
- Finally

☆ Punctuation
.
?
!

☆ Capitals only where they go
- Beginning of sentence
- Names

☆ Spelling
- All word wall words

☆ Neat and clean handwriting

Tiered Vocabulary

I	II	III	
EVERYBODY	**EDUCATED PEOPLE**	**EXPERTS:**	
do	able	employee:	competent
above	upper	snob:	utmost
across	crossways	police:	intersection
scared	afraid	Wizard of Oz:	cowardly
past	ago	teacher:	history
in front	ahead	clerk:	forward
air	breeze	scientist:	atmosphere
just about	almost	teacher:	nearly
always	constantly	doctor:	regularly
mad	angry	actor:	livid
answer	reply, solve	scientist:	solution
anyone	anybody	teacher	whomever
anything	any item	kids' slang:	whatever
house	apartment	realtor:	condominium
arm	limb	doctor:	extremity
sleeping	asleep	zoologist:	dormant, hibernate
ate	eaten	doctor:	consumed

Tiered Vocabulary – Multiple Meaning

I	II	III	
EVERYBODY	**EDUCATED PEOPLE**	**EXPERTS**	
make	build	architect:	erects
	create	scientist:	invents
	type	car salesman:	style
	earn	parents:	acquire
	bring about	lawyer:	cause
good	kind	teacher:	thoughtful, considerate
	able	carpenter:	expert
	interesting	movie goer:	thrilling
	polite	parents:	well-behaved, well-mannered
	fine	antique dealer:	perfect, undamaged
break	crack	nurse/doctor:	fracture
	pause, rest	movie goer:	intermission
	not follow	parents:	disobey
clear	see-through	artist:	transparent
	simple	writer:	uncomplicated, straight-forward
	obvious	lawyer:	evident

Tiered Vocabulary

I	II	III	
EVERYBODY	**EDUCATED PEOPLE**	**EXPERTS:**	

Academic Language Sentence Stems
Standards-Based

These formats are all available on the CD, for grades 2-6 for Math and English/Language Arts. The words are based on the California Standards Test (CST) academic language students are expected to understand for each grade level.

California Standards Based Academic Language
Grade 3 English Language Arts

Here are phrases that can be used to help students become familiar with the language of the standards-based testing for that grade level. Students need to be able to read and understand what is being asked about reading passages on tests using these kinds of terms and phrases. Teachers can use these in everyday teaching to get students used to hearing and using these terms.

Word Analysis	
word sentence spelled meaning different(ly) divide syllable author dictionary entry passage vowel sound underlined part correct noun verb adjective adverb synonym letter form pair antonym main heading suffix group include rhyme	• What does the word _____ mean in this sentence? • In this sentence you can tell that a _____ is: • Which of the following words from this sentence could be spelled differently and have a different meaning? • How should the word _____ be divided into syllables? • In the sentence above, the author uses the word _____ to show that: • Which dictionary entry gives the BEST meaning for the word _____ as it is used in the sentence in the box? • Which word has the same vowel sound as the underlined part of _____? • What is the correct way to divide _____ into syllables? • Which word is a SYNONYM for _____ as it is used in the sentence? • The word _____ ends in _____. Which one of these letters can be added to _____ to form another words. • Which pair of words makes the sentence correct? • Which word is an ANTONYM for _____? • Which two words are ANTONYMS? • Which word is a main heading for the other three words? • Which of the following suffixes can be added at the end of the word _____ to make a new word that means "someone who

STANDARDS OVERVIEW for the WEEK of _____

READING/LANGUAGE ARTS

Word Analysis: _____

Reading Comprehension: _____

Literary Analysis: _____

Written Conventions: _____

Writing Strategies: _____

Writing Applications: _____

MATHEMATICS

Number Sense 1 & 2: _____

Number Sense 3 & 4: _____

Algebra & Functions: _____

Measurement & Geometry: _____

Statistics: _____

Kidified Standards R/LA & Math K-6

These checklists are complete renditions of the California State Standards for English Language Arts and Math, which have been "kidified" for easier understanding by students. These checklists are available on the CD provided with this book. Here is a sample page.

Grade 1		Week 1	Week 2	Week 3	Week 4	Week 5	Week 6
Word Analysis, Fluency, and Systematic Vocabulary Development							
1.0	Students understand the basic features of reading.						
Concepts About Print							
1.1	I can match words that I hear to words that I see.						
1.2	I can find the title and author of a story.						
1.3	I can find letters, words, and sentences.						
Phonemic Awareness							
1.4	I can hear sounds in words.						
1.5	I know the short and long vowel sounds.						
1.6	I can make rhyming words.						
1.7	I can play with sounds in words. By changing letters I can make new words.						
1.8	I can blend sounds.						
1.9	I know all the sounds in a word.						
Decoding and Word Recognition							
1.10	I know the sounds and how to use them to spell them correctly.						
1.11	I can read my word wall words.						
1.12	I can use the sound/spelling cards to read words with special spellings.						
1.13	I can read compound words and contractions.						
1.14	I can read words with special endings.						
1.15	I know word families.						
1.16	I can read books aloud in a voice that others understand.						
1.17	I can sort words that are alike.						
Reading Comprehension							
2.0	Students read and understand grade-level-appropriate material.						
Structural Features of Informational Materials							
2.1	I can understand the order of a story						
Comprehension and Analysis of Grade-Level-Appropriate Text							
2.2	I can tell who is in a story and what happened in a story.						
2.3	I can follow written directions.						

Data Walls

These are available in their original size on the CD with this booklet and are modifiable.

Student Score Cards XLS

Class Proficiency Charts

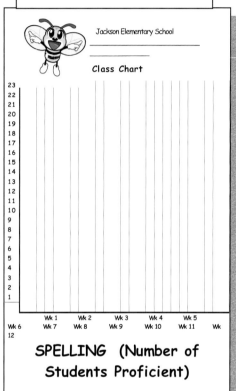

Jackson Elementary School

_____

Class Chart

SPELLING (Number of Students Proficient)

Student Scorecard

Name:	Week 1			Week 2			Week 3			Week 4		
Date:	Goal	% Correct	Goal Met Y/N	Goal	% Correct	Goal Met Y/N	Goal	% Correct	Goal Met Y/N	Goal	% Correct	Goal Met Y/N
Reading Comprehension												
Vocabulary												
Spelling												
Math												
Fluency												
Homework 4 pt Rubric												
Conduct 4 pt Rubric												

Homework Rubric:
4: complete, neat, on time
3: complete, on time
2: incomplete
1: incomplete/late

" . . . [Success is] trying to be the best you can be!
Don't worry what others may have or might say.
When trying your best,
Success comes your way."
Inch and Miles: The Journey to Success, John R. Wooden

MISSION 350!

TO PROFICIENT AND BEYOND

Colors Mission 350 and Beyond

PROFICIENT = 350+

BASIC = 300+

BELOW BASIC

FAR BELOW BASIC

BENCHMARK TEACHER TEST CHAT

Teacher's Name: Grade:

CURRENT BENCHMARK: WHAT WERE YOUR 2 STRONGEST AREAS IN (use *CLASSROOM EXAM REPORT*):
  ❖ Language Arts:
  ❖ Math:

To what Instructional Strategies do you attribute this?
  ➢ _____
  ➢ _____

How many students are currently at grade level . . .

How many will be at grade level . . .

	Current Data	Goal for Next Year BENCHMARK:_____	Goal for this Year
ENGLISH			
MATH			

WHICH 10 STUDENTS SCORED THE MAJORITY IN BASIC (Yellow) IN ELA?

(USE *PERFORMANCE SUMMARY REPORT*)

1	2	3	4	5
6	7	8	9	10

WHAT ARE YOU GOING TO DO DIFFERENTLY TO HELP YOUR TARGET STUDENTS MOVE UP TO PROFICIENT?:
  ➢ _____
  ➢ _____
  ➢ _____

WHAT SUPPORT CAN ADMINISTRATION AND RESOURCE PROVIDE TO HELP YOUR STUDENTS ACHIEVE?:
  ➢ _____
  ➢ _____

MY SCORES, MY TARGETS

NAME_____

TEACHER_____ GRADE_____

TEST	2007		2008		DIFFERENCE	GOAL FOR 2009	
CST -ELA	SS	Level	SS	Level		SS	Level
CST -Math	SS	Level	SS	Level		SS	Level
CELDT	SS Level		SS	Level		SS	Level
Writing							

What am I going to work harder on this year?

Reading, language arts, spelling, writing
  ➤
  ➤

Math
  ➤
  ➤

Other?

TEST CHAT: Elementary

CALIFORNIA STANDARDS TEST (CST) & THE CELDT

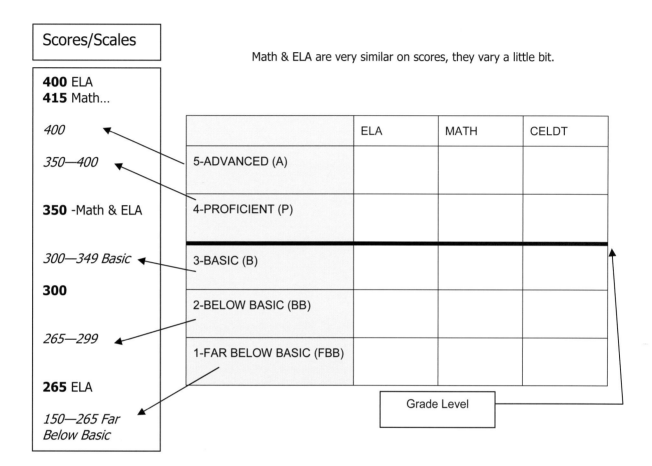

Scores/Scales

400 ELA
415 Math...

400

350—400

350 -Math & ELA

300—349 Basic

300

265—299

265 ELA

150—265 Far Below Basic

Math & ELA are very similar on scores, they vary a little bit.

	ELA	MATH	CELDT
5-ADVANCED (A)			
4-PROFICIENT (P)			
3-BASIC (B)			
2-BELOW BASIC (BB)			
1-FAR BELOW BASIC (FBB)			

Grade Level

How did I do last year?

What is my goal for this year in English language arts and math?

What am I going to do differently this year in order to meet my goals?
  ➢ at home:
  ➢ at school:

Other Data Sheets

These are available in their original size on the CD with this booklet and are modifiable.

2nd Cold Read Bookmarks

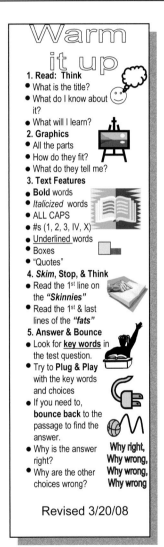

Warm it up

1. Read: Think
- What is the title?
- What do I know about it?
- What will I learn?

2. Graphics
- All the parts
- How do they fit?
- What do they tell me?

3. Text Features
- **Bold** words
- *Italicized* words
- ALL CAPS
- #s (1, 2, 3, IV, X)
- Underlined words
- Boxes
- "Quotes"

4. *Skim*, Stop, & Think
- Read the 1st line on the *"Skinnies"*
- Read the 1st & last lines of the *"fats"*

5. Answer & Bounce
- Look for **key words** in the test question.
- Try to **Plug & Play** with the key words and choices
- If you need to, **bounce back** to the passage to find the answer.
- Why is the answer right? **Why right,**
- Why are the other choices wrong? **Why wrong, Why wrong, Why wrong**

Revised 3/20/08

Scholar Math Vocabulary Chart

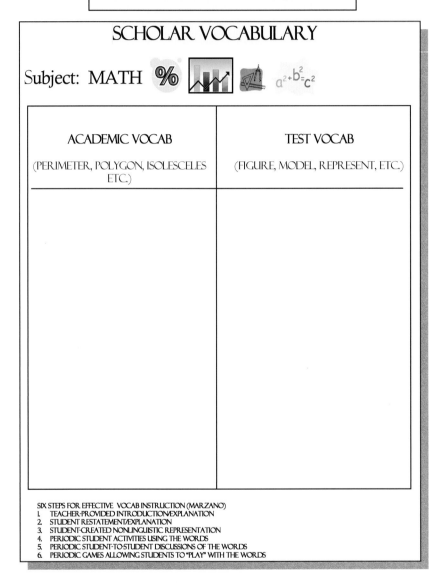

SCHOLAR VOCABULARY

Subject: MATH $a^2 + b^2 = c^2$

ACADEMIC VOCAB (PERIMETER, POLYGON, ISOLESCELES ETC.)	TEST VOCAB (FIGURE, MODEL, REPRESENT, ETC.)

SIX STEPS FOR EFFECTIVE VOCAB INSTRUCTION (MARZANO)
1. TEACHER-PROVIDED INTRODUCTION/EXPLANATION
2. STUDENT RESTATEMENT/EXPLANATION
3. STUDENT-CREATED NONLINGUISTIC REPRESENTATION
4. PERIODIC STUDENT ACTIVITIES USING THE WORDS
5. PERIODIC STUDENT-TO-STUDENT DISCUSSIONS OF THE WORDS
6. PERIODIC GAMES ALLOWING STUDENTS TO "PLAY" WITH THE WORDS

Skill and Will Matrix

GUIDE

Invest time early on
- Coach and train
- Answer questions/explain

Create a risk-free environment to allow early mistakes/learning.

Relax control as progress is shown

DELEGATE

Provide freedom to do the job
- Set objective, not method
- Praise, don't ignore

Encourage coachee to take responsibility.
- Involve in decision-making
- Use "You tell me what you think."

Take appropriate risks
- Give more stretching tasks
- Don't over-manage

DIRECT

First build the will
- Provide clear briefing
- Identify motivations
- Develop a vision of future performance
- Structure tasks for quick win

Then build the skill
- Coach and train
- Provide frequent feedback

Then sustain the skill
- Praise and nurture
- Supervise closely with clear rules

EXCITE

Identify the reason for low will

Motivate
- Create assignments that foster discovery
- Align with student curiosity
- Encourage/invite service to others

Monitor, feedback

	HIGH WILL	LOW WILL
LOW SKILL	GUIDE / DIRECT	
HIGH SKILL	DELEGATE / EXCITE	

HIGH WILL

LOW WILL

LOW SKILL

HIGH SKILL

Adaptation from The Tao of Coaching, Boost Your Effectiveness at Work By Inspiring Those Around You. Max Landsberg, Knowledge Exchange, LLC Santa Monica pp 144-145

The Testing Word Cards

We have developed "word cards" for both California Standards Test (CST) testing language and future-oriented college or career language. These cards provide teachers with accurate visual prompts that will generate or stimulate an action appropriate to each context.

Use of these cards is aligned with current scientific research placing high value on non-linguistic representations (NLRs) in teaching. (Marzano, 2005). Used as non-linguistic representations, these Word Cards especially serve **new readers**, **slow decoders**, and **English language learners**.

The Testing Word Cards

These word cards are designed from the specific language used in the California Standards Test (CST).

They can be used...

- **To accelerate comprehension and student responses**
- **to enhance the understanding of testing language; or**
- **as simple flash cards for words and phrases students need to remember in any context.**

Here are some pictures of word cards you will find on the CD in this book.

Each card is 8-1/2X11 format or can be modified.

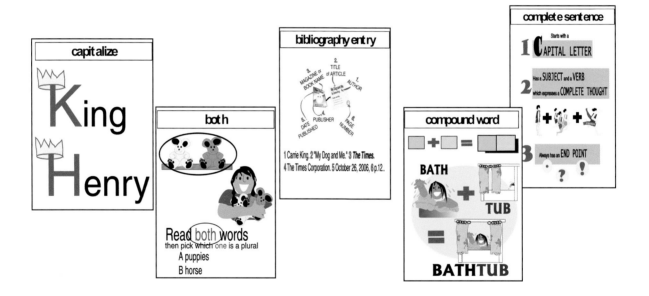

REMEMBER

The ability to restate, recall, and recognize previously learned material. You think about what was important and write it down.

Tell Name Locate Describe Identify

Explain Retell Define List Memorize

Label Find Match

Who, what, why, where, when?

Name all the characters in the story.

How would you describe...?

Can you list three _____?

Write six facts from the story.

When/where does the story take place?

How does the story end?

UNDERSTAND

The ability to make sense of material. To grasp the meaning of information you have learned.

You do this by looking at what you learned from a variety of perspectives.

Interpret	Exemplify	Summarize	Classify
Infer	Paraphrase	Compare	Explain
Outline	Discuss	Illustrate	Restate
Demonstrate	Describe	Compare	Contrast

Will you restate in your own words?

What facts or ideas show...?

Can you explain what is meant...?

How would you rephrase the meaning...?

What is the main idea of...?

Can you explain what is happening...?

How would you summarize...?

Which is the best answer...?

APPLY

The ability to use learned material in new situations.

You use varied concepts, methods, and theories to do this.

Implement   Carry out   Use   Construct

Execute   Translate   Demonstrate   Adapt

Solve   Organize   Practice   Build

Calculate   Tabulate   Change

Using what you learned, how would you solve...?

How would you show your understanding of...?

What questions would you ask in an interview with...?

How would you use...?

What examples can you find to...?

How would you organize _____ to show...?

What elements would you choose to change...?

ANALYZE

The ability to break material into many components so that its structures may be understood. You identify parts, examine the relationships of the parts to each other and to the whole, and recognize the organizational principles involved.

Compare   Contrast   Organize   Outline   Infer

Deconstruct   Structure   Conclude   Argue   Debate

Question   Detect   Distinguish   Defend   Investigate

Examine   Categorize

What are the parts or features of....?

What is the motive...?

What inference can you make?

What conclusions can you draw?

How would you classify?

How would you categorize?

What evidence can you find?

EVALUATE

The ability to judge the value of the material based on specific criteria and standards.

You conduct assessments from a variety of perspectives.

Check   Hypothesize Critique Test
Experiment   Judge   Detect   Monitor
Assess   Appraise   Justify   Dispute
Evaluate   Decide   Select   Question
Opinion   Agree/disagree   Prove/disprove Prioritize

Do you agree with the actions...?

How would you prove/disprove...?

How would you prioritize the facts...?

What is your opinion of...?

What would you cite to defend the actions...?

What choice would you have made...?

How would you evaluate...?

Page 141

CREATE

The ability to put parts together to form a plan that is new. It may involve the production of a unique communication (essay/speech) or a plan of operations, (research proposal).

You can reframe information into something entirely new.

Design	Construct	Invent	Make		
Plan	Produce	Devise	Imagine		
Compose	Create	Infer	Estimate		
Formulate	Propose	Modify	Improve/change		

What changes would you make to solve...?

What would happen if...?

Can you propose an alternative...?

What could be combined to improve/change...?

What way would you design...?

How would you estimate the results for...?

How would you change/modify the plot...? Why?

BLOOM'S TAXONOMY

1. REMEMBER	2. UNDERSTAND

3. APPLY	4. ANALYZE

5. EVALUATE	6. CREATE

The College and Career Word Cards

There are 45 word cards designed for discussing future orientation, secondary education, career, technical school, and other future choices. The cards provide teachers with accurate visual prompts for life choices that may be unfamiliar for students.

Note the pictures of the word cards you will find on the CD in this book. Each card is 8-1/2X11 format or can be modified.

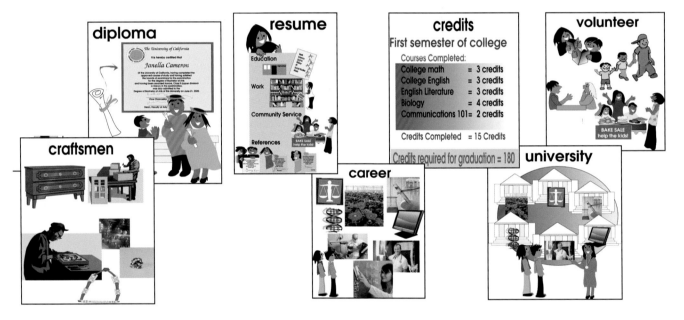

The "Middle School"
Forms and Icons

From Portrait of a Middle School Classroom

All of the following forms and icons for middle school goals and strategies discussed in "Portrait of a Middle School Classroom" are also available on the CD.

The Big Goal Award is on the CD

©Kilian Betlach

BIG GOAL #1
Improve writing score 1 point

Summary

	1	**2**	**3**	**4**

Persuasive

	1	**2**	**3**	**4**

Response

	1	**2**	**3**	**4**

©Kilian Betlach

BIG GOAL #2
MASTER 80% of all skills

100%				
90%				
80%				
70%				
60%				
50%				
40%				
30%				
20%				
10%				
0%				

BIG GOAL #3
Raise reading score 2 grade levels

BIG GOAL #4
Read 180 words per minute

220	
210	
200	
190	
180	
170	
160	
150	
140	
130	
120	
110	
100	
90	
80	
70	
60	
50	
40	
30	
20	
10	

☐ **Fiction**   ☐ **Non-fiction**

©Kilian Betlach

READING NON-FICTION
Types of Media

Title	Type	Topic
Author	**Audience**	**Author's Purpose**

Title	Type	Topic
Author	**Audience**	**Author's Purpose**

Title	Type	Topic
Author	**Audience**	**Author's Purpose**

READING NON-FICTION
Text Features

Title:	Genre:
Pages:	

Pictures/ Diagrams	Description/ Predication
Text Boxes	**Prediction/ Confirmation**
Headings	**Questions**
Connection	**Justification**

STARTER/ CLOSER

Week of ☐ **to** ☐

Monday

[*starter*]
[*closer*]

Tuesday

[*starter*]
[*closer*]

Previous vocabulary words I need to study and relearn

word	*definition*

Wednesday

[*starter*]

[*closer*]

Thursday

[*starter*]

[*closer*]

Friday

[*starter*]

[*closer*]

ACTIVE READER STRATEGIES

3 in 1

Title: **Type/ Genre:**   **Topic:**

Author: **Audience:**   **Author's Purpose:**

ASK QUESTIONS	VISUALIZE	MAKE PREDICTION
Above: Below:	 Key words:	 Confirm:
PARAPHRASE	**CAUSE & EFFECT**	**CAUSE & EFFECT**
Author's sentence: Your sentence:	Cause: Effect:	Cause: Effect:
FACT & OPINION	**CAUSE & EFFECT**	**P.O.V.**
Fact: Opinion:	Cause: Effect:	 Justification:

©Kilian Betlach

READING STRATEGIES GOAL SHEET
Reading is Thinking…

MASTER	9	8	7	6	5	4	3	2	1	
										Question
										Visualize
										Predict
										Paraphrase
										Fact & Opinion
										Make a Connection
										Cause & Effect
										Main Idea / Detail

©Kilian Betlach